easy PATIOS
& SMALL GARDENS

COLLINS

easy

PATIOS
& SMALL GARDENS

Richard Jackson
&
Carolyn Hutchinson

HarperCollins*Publishers*

Acknowledgements

The publishers thank the following for their kind permission to
reproduce the photographs in this book:

Agriframes page 40 (left), **Gillian Beckett** pages 49 (bottom), 52, 54, 88 (top), 89 (bottom), 90 (top),
96 (bottom), 97 (top right), 100 (bottom right), 101 (top), 102 (bottom left and right), 103 (top left and bottom),
104, 105 (top right and bottom), 107, 111 (bottom), 112, 113 (middle and right); **Forest Fencing Ltd** page 31;
Holt Studios pages 59 (Rosemary Mayer), 120, 122 (bottom) (Nigel Cattlin); **Hozelock** pages 83,
90 (bottom), 123 (bottom); **Natural Image** pages 21, 69, 73, 86, 97 (bottom), 100 (top), 105 (top left),
106 (right), 107 (top), 111 (top), 117 (bottom) (Bob Gibbons); 25 (top), 75 (bottom) (Liz Gibbons);
72 (top) (Chris Hart-Davies); 94 (Robin Fletcher); 108 (left) (Peter Wilson);
John Glover Photography pages 1, 6, 9 (top), 11, 17 (bottom), 20 (top), 23, 25 (bottom),
35, 36, 42, 50 (top right), 51, 55, 56, 57 (bottom), 62, 63, 64, 70, 71, 72 (bottom), 73, 79 (bottom),
84, 85, 87, 89 (top), 93 (middle and bottom), 94 (top left and bottom), 95, 96 (top), 97 (top left),
98, 99, 100 (top right), 101 (bottom left and right), 102 (top), 106 (left), 108 (right), 109, 110,
113 (left), 115 (top left, middle and right) 116; **Graham Strong Garden Folio** pages 12, 22, 23 (top),
82, 114, 115 (bottom), 117; **Suttons Seeds** page 99; **The Garden Picture Library** pages 30 (John Miller),
34 (bottom) (JS Sira), 40 (right) (Lynne Brotchie), 41, 68 (Howard Rice), 88 (bottom) (Mel Watson);
Traditional Garden Supply Company Ltd page 75 (top).

Front cover photograph of Richard Jackson by Tiggy Elliot.
All other photographs supplied by *Garden Answers* magazine.

First published as *How to Win at Patios and Small Gardens*
in 1997 by HarperCollins*Publishers*, London
This edition first published in 1999

3 5 7 9 8 6 4 2

ISBN 0 00 414056 7
Designed and produced by Cooling Brown
Colour reproduction by Colourscan, Singapore
Printed and bound in Italy by Rotolito Lombarda SpA, Milan

The HarperCollins*Publishers* website address is:
www.**fire**and**water**.com

Contents

Introduction

This new book, the latest in the 'How to Win' series, offers some quite brilliant ideas for small gardens and provides the gardener with all they need to know to create a huge impact in the smallest of spaces. There are affordable planting suggestions for mini borders – guaranteed to pack a punch! – plus tips on how to make room on the patio for pots of plants, and even a pond, as well as people.

The authors use their wealth of knowledge and experience to show how to lay the foundations for a great garden and achieve results quickly. Their enthusiastic and straightforward writing is not only an inspiration but also a pleasure to read.

Armed with this book, all gardeners – whatever their level of knowledge – will find it easy to make their garden a colourful oasis all year round. Your garden will become a great place to work, rest and play – whether it's big or small!

ADRIENNE WILD
EDITOR
Garden Answers magazine

Design

Even the simplest, most formal layout such as this hexagon can create tremendous interest and impact.

Designing a patio or small garden can sound like a bit of an undertaking, especially if you're a first-time gardener, but it's really just a progression of logical steps. We've both had a go at DIY design, by making changes to our own gardens. Nothing spectacular, nothing that would win prizes; just features that we, personally, enjoy. Adding a raised bed to a patio, putting up a pergola, terracing a slope. And we reckon that if we can do it, so can you.

The thing to bear in mind is that you're creating something special, putting your own stamp on one small piece of earth. So, right from the start, plan for a patio or garden in which you'll feel thoroughly comfortable. Let it reflect your needs, your interests, your enthusiasms and your style.

Whether you're starting with a completely empty plot attached to a brand new house, a mature garden that you've just taken over, or you simply want to give a new look to the patio or garden you've had for years, the same logic, and the same practical steps apply. So have a go – the end result will suit you down to the ground.

DESIGNING THE SMALL GARDEN
STEP 1: PLANNING
Assessing the existing plot

The first step in garden design – the planning, should be a leisurely one. Take your time and let your ideas mature.

This is especially important if you've just inherited an established garden. Ideally, you should take a full year to get to know the plants so that you can judge which to keep and which to sacrifice in your redesign. Assess the merits of each plant because in a small garden they really need to earn their keep. That forsythia, for

Take time when planning your garden. The final plan may not be up to landscape architect standards, but mapping out changes really does help to clarify your ideas.

instance, may be a jolly picture for three weeks each spring, but what's it doing for the rest of the time? Not a lot, we suspect, and it may be better to remove it.

Be very careful, though, about threatening any established trees with the chop unless they're quite obviously too tall and vigorous for the situation, or they're blocking a view that you want to open up. Mature trees with attractive foliage, blossom or bark are a valuable asset in any garden, giving height and a feeling of stability and permanence; something that would take decades to create from scratch. In a shady garden, they can add

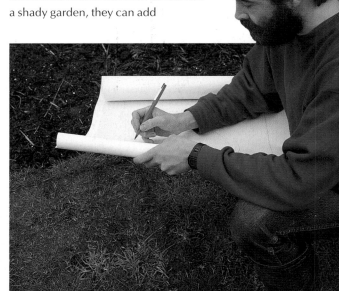

WRITING OUT A SHOPPING LIST

Decide what you want from your garden. Will it be primarily a space for entertaining friends in summer? Somewhere for the kids to play? A private retreat? Do you need room for fruit and vegetables? Because all this dictates the elements you'll need to incorporate into your design. So make a checklist:

Patio

Lawn

Shed

Greenhouse

Water feature

Vegetable and fruit area

Space for dustbins and compost bin

Don't worry too much at this stage about vertical features like pergolas, arches or screens, or about lighting – it's allocating space on the ground that's important initially. But remember, if the budget is tight, it's the paving, paths and structures that eat up the money. Lawns and plants for beds and borders cost very little by comparison.

immeasurably to a quiet, woodland atmosphere. In a sunny garden that traps every drop of summer heat, there's the additional benefit that they'll cast a welcome shade – for you, and for all those plants that hate to be in the full glare of the sun. So, woodsman, spare that tree, if at all possible. Reshape it, by all means, by thinning out an over-bushy canopy or removing a few lower branches so that you can actually stand, rather than crouch, under it; but think long and hard before you remove it.

Drawing up a plan

Having assessed the value of any existing plants (a pretty quick job in a new garden where only builders' rubble flourishes), the next step is to draw up a plan.

First make a rough sketch, marking in:

- The boundaries
- The portion of the house that adjoins the garden, noting the position of doors and windows
- Existing features such as lawn, beds, paths, shed, trees and large shrubs
- Any slopes
- Immovable objects like manhole covers and oil storage tanks

You should also note the position of any bad views that you want to screen, and any that you want to keep. There might, for instance, be a particularly fine tree in a neighbouring garden that you could cunningly incorporate into your own garden picture. Finally, indicate the sunny spots, shady corners and any windy spots that would benefit from extra screening.

Now measure up the garden, noting the measurements on the rough sketch. This can then be transferred to graph paper, with each set of ten squares representing, say, one square metre or square yard, marking all outlines in bold black ink.

Transferring your ideas to paper

Now take your plan, and place tracing paper over it, or a sheet of clear acetate. Use a pencil and rubber for the tracing paper and a wipe-off marker pen for the acetate.

First mark in any features that you're keeping or, like the manhole cover, are stuck with, then start to allocate space for the essential features from your shopping list, remembering that:

a) Greenhouses and fruit and vegetable plots must be in the sun, lawns much prefer a sunny spot, and you'll also probably want the patio to be in sun for as much of the day as possible.

b) Sheds, compost bins and dustbins are not too beautiful, and will benefit from being tucked away in a quiet corner where they can be screened off from the rest of the garden.

You may find, at this stage, that you've been a bit ambitious about what can be fitted in and that some of your chosen extra features will have to go. But you can compromise – fruit and vegetables, for instance, can be incorporated into the general garden plantings, while if a free-standing greenhouse is gobbling up too much space, there may be room for a little lean-to greenhouse against a sunny wall. There are also small lean-to sheds that tuck neatly against a wall or fence, and it's not as if you're going to need room for a ride-on mower and a vast armoury of equipment for a small garden.

Once you've marked the positions of the main features, try out a few design ideas remembering the cardinal rule that's so important in any garden, but crucial in a small one: keep it **strong and simple**. A fiddly, distracting design makes for a fiddly, distracting garden that's all at sixes and sevens with itself.

A few other important points to remember: paths should be functional; they may also, incidentally, be very beautiful, but it's essential that they take a logical

route. A meandering path through a lawn for instance, may look pretty, but no-one's actually going to use it and you'll soon find a secondary short-cut path engraved in the grass. A patio needs to be big enough to comfortably accommodate table, chairs and possibly a barbecue and a few attractive planted pots. Children's play areas should be within sight of the house.

Once the main ground features are in place, sketch in the position of any vertical features such as arches, screens and pergolas.

After much drawing and redrawing, you'll finally hit on a design that pleases, and seems to suit all your needs. But again, don't rush, take time to check that it really is going to work.

Reinforcing your ideas

Minor changes to an existing garden are easy to mark out on the ground, to check whether they're going to be effective. If you're reshaping the lawn, for instance, use a length of hosepipe (curved lawn) or pegs and string (square or rectangle). A couple of bamboo poles lashed together can stand in for a tree, a dustbin lid for a tiny pool and more bamboo canes can be mocked up into an archway. And to get an idea of the finished effect, look at the garden from the house windows, both upstairs and down; this 'overview' will help you to spot, and adjust, any part of the picture that doesn't work.

More radical changes are virtually impossible to mark out on the ground, unless you're starting with a completely empty plot. So use the photograph trick. Take photographs of the entire garden, from all angles, and most especially from the house windows (up and down again) and from any proposed patio or sitting area. And to give you decent-sized pictures to work from, get them blown up on a photocopier to A4 size.

Now place sheets of acetate over the pictures and mark in the changes; you needn't be too precise, just the main lines of the alterations, and a few billowing shapes for shrubs, mop-headed lollipops for trees. You'll be

A strong, simple plan that will look equally good in winter, using contrasting shapes and textures of paving and an attractive backdrop of evergreens.

astonished at how clearly it shows the effect of your proposed changes, and where any weaknesses lie. So that once you've made any necessary adjustments, you can set about turning your plan into a reality with complete confidence.

STEP 2: GETTING TO WORK

Simple changes to the garden, such as altering the shape of a lawn or installing a water feature, are easy to implement. But if you're going the whole hog and revamping the entire garden, or creating one from scratch, there's a logical sequence of events to be followed.

1) Start with the 'bones' of your plan; the paths,

If you're starting with a completely empty plot, it's easy to mark out your proposed design, using pegs and string. For curved designs, you could peg down lengths of hosepipe.

It sounds a bit didactic, but if you did it the other way round, you'd dig up the bulbs by mistake while you were planting the hardy perennials, you wouldn't be able to find room for the shrubs because you'd gone a bit mad with the herbs and roses, and you'd discover that the ideal spot for a tree is just where you'd painstakingly planted a conifer.

STEP 4: THE FINISHING TOUCHES

A garden is a bit like a room, and now that it's fully furnished, you can start adding in the 'ornaments'; planted pots and hanging baskets, a birdbath, a statue, an ornate bench. Which brings us to the topic of focal points, which we've touched on only briefly so far.

A focal point can be any striking feature, from a tree to a handsome urn, that will draw the eye and give the garden a unified, restful feel. Your planted pots, birdbath, statue etc. will certainly qualify, so place them with care. Use them as a pleasing contrast; an urn

patios and paved areas. If you're installing lighting, put cable conduits in at this stage so that they run below paths and paving rather than having to be snaked round them later.

2) Repair or replace any boundary fences if necessary.

3) Install any permanent structures such as a shed, greenhouse or pergola.

Follow the book through and you'll find advice and useful step-by-step sequences on all these hard landscaping elements.

STEP 3: PLANTING

Now the groundwork's done, you're left with the spaces in-between, and it's time to get planting. After, of course, you've made sure that your soil is in good condition, and chosen all the very best plants for your particular soil and aspect (see 'Plants and Planting').

Again, there's a logical sequence to it, starting with trees. They'll be one of the most dominant features of any small garden, so it's important to put them in first so that you can build the surrounding plantings around them.

Even though they're marked down for a particular spot on your plan, do double-check that you've got the siting right, especially if you're using a tree to screen a bad view. Choose the spot from which the view most offends (an outdoor dining area perhaps, or a house window), and make sure that the tree is slap-bang in front of the eyesore.

Slot the climbers, shrubs and conifers in next, following on with roses, herbs, hardy perennials and, finally, bulbs.

Permanent structures such as this handsome little summerhouse can add real style to the garden.

Plants are a vital part of your 'garden architecture', so plan for plenty of contrasts of colour, texture and form.

planted with bright summer bedding plants against a dark green background, or a spiky yucca exploding from a soft-leaved underplanting. As an invitation to explore; a small statue marking the entrance to a part of the garden that's hidden from view. Or to emphasise the transition from one part of the garden to another; two planted pots, for instance, to flank the start of a pathway, or the top of a flight of steps.

Remember, like your overall design, keep it simple and don't overdo it. Never put two focal points close together (they'll cancel each other out), and don't incorporate too many in the overall design or you'll be giddy from trying to take them all in.

A simple pot, like this rhubarb forcer, makes a handsome focal point in the happy jumble of a cottage garden border.

TIPS

✔ *To give a feeling of space, be generous in the plantings against your boundary walls or fences. Physical barriers are a clear indication of the extent of the garden, but once they're swamped in foliage, it's virtually impossible to tell – giving the illusion that the garden is much larger than it actually is.*

✔ *Rather than being able to take in the whole of your garden at one glance, make it more interesting by creating at least one area that's not immediately visible. We're not talking about the screened-off dustbins here, but the principle's the same. Set up a panel of wide-mesh trellis, for instance, and plant it with a not too vigorous climber, to give you an intriguing and enticing glimpse of the garden beyond.*

✔ *In addition to your major ornamental features, plan a few surprises, so that a tour round the garden is full of extra interest. But keep them low key, so that people really do have to explore to find them. A sleeping stone cat tucked into a sunny corner, for instance, or a terracotta tortoise snacking among the lettuces.*

DESIGNING A PATIO GARDEN

If your garden is so tiny that the only sensible option is to pave it over, then it's a patio garden. Or you could call it a 'courtyard' – a lovely word that conjures up images of white-washed Mediterranean gardens dripping with bougainvillea. Whatever you call it, the aim is to create a feeling of tranquillity and seclusion – a quiet retreat swathed in foliage and flowers. This is especially important in small town gardens, because all those leaves deflect a terrific amount of noise and pollution.

Many of the design 'rules' for creating a small garden apply equally well to the patio garden, with 'keep it simple' at the top of the list. An over-complex pattern of paving, for instance, will be distracting. Similarly, cluster pots together rather than dotting them about, in groups of complementary materials; terracotta and plastic, for example, don't always look good together.

Exploit the space's potential to the full by incorporating raised beds – they're a terrific option for the patio garden. They provide an interesting change of level and need much less upkeep than pots because of the sheer volume of compost they hold. They also extend the range of plants you can grow, because you can invest in some of the lovely trailers that would sprawl on the ground when grown in pots – a ground cover rose like 'Snow Carpet', for example, makes a beautiful edge-breaker.

The other great trick when planning a patio garden is to anchor it firmly to the house – if the two can be persuaded to merge together, the eye fools the brain into thinking that the space is larger than it actually is. At its simplest, planting up the house walls, and making sure that your patio can be admired from indoors, will do the job. Or you could go for something more structural – a pergola, built over house windows and planted up, will blur the division between indoors and out.

The 'freehand' design and mixed materials in the paving of this small patio garden could be distracting, but they're unified by the use of muted shades of grey.

On very shady patios, lighten the gloom by painting walls and fences white and using light-coloured paving. Full-length mirrors, shrouded in foliage, will also add a sparkle, with the bonus that they can trick you into thinking that they're a doorway, making the space seem that much bigger. The longest lasting are heavy duty mirrors (at least 6mm/¼in thick), and you can give added weather protection by sealing the edges with waterproof tape. A similar effect can be created by fixing ornamental 'trompe l'oeuil' trellis to the walls; it gives an illusion of depth, and also looks good when deciduous wall plants have died back.

Think, too, about the use you're going to make of the patio. You may like to do a lot of entertaining – so make sure there's plenty of room for table, chairs and barbecue, and keep a few pots of herbs close by the kitchen door for ultra-fresh last minute garnishes. Perhaps you have young children who, if there isn't room for a swing, would enjoy a sand pit that can later be turned into a little scree garden filled with gravel and alpines. You could even get the children involved

Fully furnished, and beautifully tended, this patio garden packs lots of interesting features into a small space without looking fussy or overcrowded.

in the garden by asking them to paint up a few pots for you – the results would certainly be original and you never know, they might even get interested in growing things in them. Or, for a sure fire winner with kids, install a little bubble fountain (see p80); it will fascinate them.

When it comes to furnishing your patio with plants, the sky's the limit. As you'll see from our container gardening chapter, all but the most vigorous plants will grow well in pots, tubs and raised beds so long as you keep them well fed and watered. Climbers will thrive, and are vital for clothing walls and disguising boundaries, making the space feel comfortable and well furnished. Small trees, too, will be happy in large pots or tubs, casting a cooling shade if the garden is a sun-trap. As in the open garden, these taller plants give a feeling of scale and permanence, gardening in three dimensions rather than two.

Climbers are an essential ingredient in the patio garden – take away the rose and rampant jasmine and this would still be a pretty scene, but much less welcoming.

TIPS

✔ *Keep the patio well manicured. In a confined space, every dead flower or straggly stem is an eyesore, so snip them out – just a few minutes work every day can ensure a picture of polished perfection.*

✔ *When you're adding the finishing touches to the patio, keep them in scale; a whacking great statue, for example, will be over-whelming.*

✔ *Scent is such an important factor in a patio garden that it's worth looking out for those plants that are extra-generous with it. Our favourites include jasmine, hyacinths, daffodils such as 'Actaea' and 'Thalia', roses (many), lilies (many), Brompton stocks, pinks (Dianthus), honeysuckle, sweet peas and 'Sensation' tobacco plants (Nicotiana).*

At the very lowest level, even the paving can be softened by planting if you engineer a few gaps – chamomile and creeping thymes smell wonderful as you brush past them, and mind-your-own-business (*Helxine/Soleirolia*) forms soft, tiny-leaved hummocks.

Between the two extremes, pack raised beds, pots and planters with a succession of colour from bulbs, bedding plants, herbaceous plants and shrubs, incorporating plenty of evergreens to keep the area interesting even in the depths of winter.

Flower colours are another factor to consider. You will need to bear in mind that although bright colours such as reds and blues are lovely during the day, they fade into the background very quickly at dusk. So add in plenty of whites and other paler colours. They'll shine on luminously through summer evenings, greatly adding to the pleasure you get from your patio. And if they're scented, so much the better. Just imagine a few pots of white lilies and nicotiana, glimmering away and breathing luscious wafts of perfume on the evening air. Magic.

DESIGN IDEAS FOR SMALL GARDENS

Free-flowing schemes

A small garden can be designed so that it contains a remarkable number of features (paved area, pergola, pool, lawn and beds, for instance) without looking overcrowded and fussy. The golden rule, as ever, is to keep the ground-plan, and the details, as strong and simple as possible, so that each feature has a chance to shine in its own right.

Putting the jigsaw together

When you're putting together a garden that contains several different features, think of it as a jigsaw. The pieces should interlock, with a natural flow from one to another. It doesn't matter whether the pieces are rounded or straight-edged – as long as they fit together comfortably, you're going to achieve a coherent picture.

If you like soft, curving lines, for instance, a semicircular patio by the house could lead on to a gently curving lawn surrounded by plantings. A small pool could be set into the border so that it follows, and echoes, the curve of the lawn.

In a more geometrical design, a few simple squares and rectangles are all you need, locked together into a grid which, while it looks very plain and formal to start with, will come to life when you soften it with plantings. You could allow your sections to overlap, to jut into one another at one or two points, creating some interesting L-shapes and a greater feeling of space.

Creating balance

In any garden, there are quiet bits (lawns, paths, paved areas), and busy bits (trees, plantings, pergolas – anything that's vertical rather than horizontal). In a small garden, in particular, it's important to get the right balance between the two, to keep the picture harmonious.

It may sound a bit pretentious, but it's just common-sense really. If, for instance, you have a tree, a pergola, an arbour and a greenhouse jostling for position it's going to look awfully cluttered. On the other hand, a patio and lawn with low surrounding plantings will look very flat and featureless.

It's simply a matter of making sure that neither element (quiet or busy), dominates the other. That way, you can enjoy and appreciate them both equally. So when you're putting together your plan, just double-check that areas occupied by busy features are balanced, roughly half and half, by quieter ones.

Keeping the details simple

Just as your overall ground-plan should be kept as simple as possible, so should the remaining details.

Take the paving, for instance. Keeping it consistent throughout the garden will hold the picture together, providing a unity that's vital in a small space. Have fun with it, by all means, by mixing materials together or by laying it in decorative patterns. But try to avoid massive contrasts in paving colour and style between one part of the garden and another – it'll give you, and the garden, the fidgets.

The lawn, too, should be as simple as possible. Any curves should be bold and generous, so avoid any temptation to wiggle. And keep the lawn free of clutter – one small tree in the centre is fine, so long as the lawn is big enough to accommodate it, but two or more will be distracting.

The same consistency should be carried through to vertical features. If you're using trellis, for instance, stick to either square mesh or diamond mesh, rather than a mixture of the two. And plan the pergola so that it echoes the paved outline below; a circular patio, for example, could be enclosed by a pergola that fans out around it and makes the whole area look so much more inviting.

An effective mix of materials in a bold layout based on interlocking squares and rectangles.

Changing direction with style. A striking bamboo screens the garden beyond, which a come-hitherish pot of petunias invites you to explore.

Changes of direction

Try to plan the garden so that at one or two points, the layout forces you to change direction, rather than being able to stride from one end to the other without interruption. Partially block one section of the garden from another with a planted bed, for instance, or with something as simple as a low hedge or trellis screen, that forces you to walk round it. The odd thing is that the garden will seem bigger (and more interesting) if it's laid out so that you walk around it, rather than simply through it.

The other change of direction is up (or down), and it has the same effect of making the garden that bit more diverse and interesting. So take advantage of any slopes, make a real feature of them, by levelling and terracing, and by incorporating steps. Harder work initially, but well worth it for the effects you can achieve.

In an entirely flat garden, you can create a change of level by incorporating raised beds, but they should always be sited so that they lock naturally into the overall design, rather than looking as though they've been tacked on. They are often most effective around the perimeter of the garden, where they'll break up the vertical lines of walls or fences and give extra height and importance to your plantings. If you're placing them more centrally, keep them lower, so that (especially when you're sitting down) they enhance the view rather than blocking it.

Formal schemes

A formal design can be tremendously effective in a small garden, because the rigid ground-plan holds the picture together and gives a feeling of ordered calm, however exuberant the plantings within it.

The key to a formal layout is symmetry and you could, for instance, take your cue from Elizabethan gardens, where the *parterre* was an essential element a stately home or manor garden. These were areas the size of several tennis courts where a stylised pattern of beds and paths was laid out like a carpet; delightful to walk through without wetting the hem of your skirt, and immensely impressive when viewed from an upstairs window. Not exactly a feasible proposition for a small garden, but it's perfectly possible to take just one element from the carpet and scale it down.

Possibly the easiest of all is the pattern that radiates

KEEPING THE COSTS DOWN IN THE FORMAL GARDEN

• Mature topiary plants (standard bays, box lollipops) can be ruinously expensive, so experiment with fast-growing *Lonicera nitida*. This is a tiny-leaved, shrubby member of the honeysuckle family, and while it's normally used for hedging, it lends itself beautifully to being clipped into more interesting shapes. You can very quickly achieve impressive spires, pyramids and balls of either the plain green form or golden-leaved 'Baggesen's Gold', which prefers a sunny spot. It will need pretty frequent clipping, but you'll find that these self-same clippings root extremely easily, and can be used to create further specimens.

• Paving is an important element in a formal design, but if the budget won't stretch to York stone or granite setts, use a simpler material in an imaginative way. Bricks, for instance, can look terrifically effective if they're laid in a herringbone or basket-weave pattern.

• Young plants of dwarf box (*Buxus sempervirens* 'Suffruticosa') can be very expensive if you buy them at the garden centre, especially when you consider that, as an edging, they should be planted at 20cm/8in intervals. So check the advertisements in gardening magazines for mail order suppliers who normally offer them rather more cheaply.

• A good alternative to box as an edging is silvery *Santolina chamaecyparissus* (cotton lavender), with its finely divided, aromatic, foliage. Plants can be set 35cm/14in apart and clipped after flowering and again in April, to keep them neat. Its medicinal properties usually earn it a place in the herb section at the garden centre, rather than among the shrubs. Planted singly, it can be clipped into an attractive dome.

out from a strong feature like a statue, a sundial or a standard rose, surrounded by a circular path. Around this are set four square or rectangular beds, scalloped out where they adjoin the central path. Take a look at any book on the history of gardening and you'll find patterns galore to inspire you.

The groundwork for a formal garden is relatively straightforward, but it's in the planting that the fun begins, because you can play around with so many ideas. First edge the beds, as the Elizabethans did, with neatly clipped low hedges – box (*Buxus*) is the easiest to keep compact, but lavender can be very pretty so long as it's sheared back by half each spring to keep it bushy and compact.

Now fill the beds. With what? Anything that takes your fancy. They could simply be filled with closely mown grass, like a set of glowing emeralds. You could plant them up with herbs, in a riotous mix, or colour-themed so that one bed is gold, another green, another grey/silver and another purple and bronze. Or you could use them just like any garden border, and provide a succession of colour from spring bulbs to lively, scented summer plants like roses, lilies, nicotianas, pinks and phlox – a lovely sumptuous display that contrasts beautifully with the restraint of the overall scheme.

The beauty of this design is that it stays strong even in winter, the pattern of paving and evergreens shining through when the majority of plants have died down.

This charming small formal garden radiates out from a strong central feature, the neat circle of box contrasting with the more exuberant border plantings.

Formal gardens ancient and modern. A pattern of low hedges (above) creates a peaceful symmetry, while the more modern garden (left) relies on crisp, clean lines for impact.

And you can extend it to suit the shape of your garden – a long narrow garden, for instance, could incorporate two designs, sticking to the same ground plan but altering details like the central feature and the nature of the plantings within the beds.

A more modern extension of this idea, which will allow you rather more space for relaxing and entertaining, is to divide a long garden into a series of compartments, each identical in shape but with different treatments. Narrow gardens are a commonplace in terraced town streets, and this is a great way of breaking them up so that you lose the 'staring down a tunnel' effect of rectangular lawn with planting confined to the edges. One compartment could have a circular lawn, say, leading to a circular paved area with a central fountain, the two separated by a partial screen of trellis or plants to either side – and though you may think this treatment will make the garden look smaller, you'll find that it emphasises the width and, surprisingly, it actually looks larger. You can keep the formal theme going by incorporating clipped evergreens (standard holly or bay, balls or spirals of box) and while the surrounding beds can be filled with cheerful mixed plantings, try to balance up any major plants; a little cherry tree to the left, for instance, should be echoed by another to the right for a really harmonious picture.

FRONT GARDENS

Small front gardens are rarely used for anything more exciting than sweeping leaves from the path, and it's certainly not an area for entertaining or relaxing. But it is your face to the world, so it's nice to keep it cheerful.

The best way of approaching the design of a front garden is to have neon flashing lights in your brain, pulsing out the words 'low maintenance'. Because while you want it to look good, you certainly won't want to spend too much time looking after it.

So, lawns are out (who wants to lug the mower through the house anyway?), along with any plants like hybrid tea roses, that need a fair amount of attention.

By far the simplest plan is to pave the area, leaving a few spaces for planting. It sounds a bit severe, but if your paving is attractive (play around with patterns and contrasting materials) it will look quite delightful once the plants have grown and softened the hard edges. And just like the back garden, it can be as informal (random spaces for plants) or as formal (a chequerboard of paving and plants, a paved circle surrounded by small beds) as the fancy takes you.

For low maintenance plants, you'll find plenty of recommendations in 'Making Life Easier', but do make sure that they're suited to the site, so that you won't be forever watering moisture-lovers or grieving over scorched shade-lovers. Choose plants like euphorbia, hosta and ferns for a shady garden. Use drought-tolerant sun-lovers for a hot spot; lavender, rock roses (cistus), hebes and a host more, including the vast majority of herbs. You could even turn the whole space over to herbs, for a beautifully scented welcome home.

Finishing touches like pots are a bit tricky in a front garden, in that they might just go walkabout via the front gate. But a hanging basket can be secured by a padlock, and pots used for specimen plants like phormiums, or for seasonal bedding, can always be concreted in.

A magnificent welcome home from a beautifully tended honeysuckle – a tough, tolerant climber that's ideal for a front-of-house position.

If you want to screen the front garden from the road and from passers-by, a hedge might seem the obvious first option, but there are a number of shrubs and small trees that will do an excellent job without needing constant clipping.

Best of all are the open, see-through plants that will act rather like trellis, giving you privacy without the 'locked-in' feeling that a tall hedge can bring. Try an amelanchier (snowy mespilus) for example, or a shrubby rowan like *Sorbus vilmorinii*, neither reaching more than 3m/10ft or so, and both supplying good blossom, berries and autumn colour. Or flowering plants such as papery-flowered rugosa rosas, growing to around 1.8m/6ft and tall, airy shrubs like elder (*Sambucus*). So much nicer than a solid screen of hedge or wall.

FRONT GARDENS

Bricks and mortar

The imaginative use of paving materials can magically transform the dullest of areas, as the before and after pictures (above and left) demonstrate.

Once you've crystallised the design for your patio or small garden, it's time to get down to the 'bricks and mortar' stage – anything from laying paving and paths to building raised beds or low walls. But before you start, think long and hard about the materials you're going to use, because they can make a substantial difference to the end result.

A patio, for instance, can be simply a series of concrete slabs – functional, but pretty dull. Yet for virtually the same cost you could lay a pattern of bricks between the slabs to achieve something that's much more exciting and interesting.

So before you start, visit garden centres and builder's yards, borrow samples, consult the manufacturers' brochures; you'll discover an incredible range of materials. Once you've made up your mind, the construction is straightforward, and you'll end up with something to take pride in. Then you'll be able to sit on your laurels and tell your admiring friends that it's the best laid plans that pay off.

The subtle colour variations in these pavers gives an attractive finish, further softened by allowing moss to grow in the gaps.

MATERIAL CONSIDERATIONS
CONCRETE PAVING SLABS

These are the most popular choice, from the standard no-frills builder's slab to the imitations of natural stone that can look amazingly authentic (the moulds are taken from the real thing and on some slabs you can even see the stonemason's chisel marks). Others are imprinted to look like groups of bricks. Only one word of caution: they're heavy, so handle with care.

When choosing slabs, don't just consult a catalogue, because the colours aren't always accurately reproduced. Visit a local stockist and borrow some samples to bring home. As a guide, try to avoid slabs that are exactly the same colour as the house. A slight contrast is best; lighter coloured slabs look good with darker walled houses, and vice versa.

The other thing to remember is that slabs tend to darken when wet, so if you live somewhere that has more than its fair share of rain, pour water over your sample slab and decide whether you like the wet-look colour too.

The finish and texture is also important. Apart from the aesthetics, some surfaces are less slippery than others, while the roughest of the natural stone imitations may be too uneven for tables and chairs and you'll be forever wedging bits of wood under them.

MATERIAL CONSIDERATIONS

The range of style, colour and size of concrete slabs is incredible, and if it leaves you feeling totally overwhelmed and spoiled for choice, there are a couple of safe options. Plain grey slabs always fit in, and can be cheered up with an interlacing or edging of brick and mellow gold 'Cotswold stone' slabs blend in well with most buildings, including brick.

BRICKS AND PAVERS

These are more expensive than slabs (and more fiddly to lay), and can look overpowering *en masse* over large areas unless they're combined with other materials. However, they're ideal for paths and for small intimate areas where they can be laid in lovely patterns like basket-weave.

The beauty of brick is in the subtle variations of tone from one to another within a single colour range, giving an instantly mellow feel to a newly-laid path or patio. And again, borrow some samples until you find the colour that blends perfectly with your house.

Be careful, though, to check that they're suitable for outdoor paving. Many house bricks can't cope with moisture and frost, and will gradually flake or even shatter. So when buying new, always ask the supplier if they're suitable, and if second-hand, check them out by twisting a coin hard on the surface. If there is no marking

Even when they're specified as a single colour (red, say), most bricks have a subtle range of colour tones which gives instant maturity and charm to a new garden.

Make the most of concrete paving slabs by combining them with other materials such as these attractive flints.

or flaking then the brick is likely to be sufficiently durable. Engineering bricks are the toughest of the lot.

Luckily, there are no such worries with pavers. These are made from concrete or clay and are very tough. Some are brick shaped, others square or hexagonal, and some even incorporate interlocking curves. Like bricks, they're useful for irregularly shaped or curved paths and patios because they are small enough to follow the curve neatly without having to be cut. Another advantage is that, because they're not mortared together, individual pieces can be lifted and re-laid quite easily; they're often called 'flexible paving' – a useful attribute if you keep changing your mind!

NATURAL STONE

Real stone costs a great deal more than any other paving material, and the standard of imitation slabs is so good that it can be difficult to tell the two apart; so why pay any more than you need to? If you want to go for the real thing, York stone is the most widely used, and is very beautiful, but the slabs vary considerably in thickness so it's quite a challenge to lay. It also attracts moss and algae, which is part of its charm but can make it quite slippery in a damp, shady spot.

GRANITE SETTS

These have a naturally rough surface that is ideal for a non-slip path. Very attractive combined with other

TIPS

✔ *Stepping stone paths through a lawn should be spaced out at an easy walking distance. Place them on the lawn to check, then leave them in place for a few days – the yellowed grass makes an excellent excavation guide. Set them level with the lawn so that you can safely skim over them with a mower.*

materials, they're extremely hard-wearing, but expensive and fiddly to lay. Imitation granite setts aren't as heavy and cost less, but don't have quite the same charm.

COBBLES

These large rounded pebbles can be used to create attractive textured designs in the garden, but they're uncomfortable to walk on, so we don't recommend them for paths. However, in a small area (surrounding a sundial or urn, for instance) they look wonderful. They're also useful for breaking up a large expanse of paving by removing one or two slabs and replacing them with cobbles, or as a narrow boundary between path and patio.

CRAZY PAVING

Crazy paving is cheap, and fine for an informal look, but laid over a large area like a patio it can start to look a bit demented. You'll be demented, too, trying to fit together a giant jigsaw, and getting a contractor to do it would cost a small fortune. So, save it for paths and for smaller areas.

Imitation granite setts can look almost as good as the real thing, especially if laid in a decorative pattern.

One of the best things about it is that if it's laid on sand, you can leave a few gaps for creeping plants like thyme and make a very pretty feature. Weeds will creep in too in the initial stages, but shouldn't be too much trouble once the legitimate occupants have established themselves.

CONCRETE

Bought in bulk and laid in one sheet, concrete is the cheapest paving material of all, but it can look awfully stark. Transform it by using bricks or pavers either to edge it or to divide it into sections.

GRAVEL

This is another fairly cheap option and can look very attractive. But it must be kept free of leaves and other garden debris, and unfortunately, there's always the possibility that local cats will adopt it as a toilet. We've been told that large grade shingle (2cm/³⁄₄in) is less appealing to them.

WOOD

Wooden decking is popular with garden designers, but not with us. It's easy to lay, especially in slab form, and should last for years, but it attracts algae and can be lethally slippery on a rainy day. Worth considering for your sun-soaked villa in paradise when you win the lottery. Sawn tree-rings are also popular for making stepping-stone paths but again, they're slippy in wet conditions and you may need to get a grip by covering them with chicken wire.

So long as it's kept clean and well raked, gravel is a handsome alternative to paving.

CONSTRUCTING YOUR PATIO

Patio paving should complement the surroundings, rather than distract from them, so a simple design is by far the most effective. Chessboard patterns, for instance, should be used with caution, and brightly coloured paving is best avoided. Bright pink, in particular, is a disaster, because it fades to an even more appalling shade in time.

In very small areas, a single type of paving will look best, although you could create a very attractive style by mixing different sizes of the same material together.

On bigger patios, you can be bolder and mix two compatible materials together. Paving slabs, for instance, can look tremendously effective if the perimeter is edged with brick. But don't use more than two materials or the design could become over-fussy and distracting.

A few practical points worth mulling over before you embark on the construction of your patio:

- If it adjoins the house, the finished level of the patio must be at least 15cm/6in below the damp proof course, and it should slope away from the house so that rainwater drains safely into the garden. A slope of 2.5cm per 2.1m/1in per 7ft is usually sufficient.
- Paving should never be laid over a manhole or drain. Buy a specially recessed manhole cover which, ingeniously, can be fitted with paving to disguise the eyesore yet can be lifted off if you ever need access to the manhole.
- If the patio leads on to a lawn then, ideally, the paved surface should be slightly lower than the grass so that you can mow up to the very edge.

TIPS

✔ *The simplest way of keeping patios clean is to scrub them vigorously with a stiff broom, wetting it with a hosepipe as you brush. If it's particularly dirty, a high pressure sprayer from the hire shop will really make it sparkle. Moss and green slime can be cleaned off with patio and path cleaners.*

✔ *It can be difficult to calculate the number of paving slabs you need, especially if you're using different sizes together. Drawing a plan on graph paper (or on the planning grids thoughtfully supplied in some manufacturer's brochures) will help to work it out, and to be on the safe side, add an extra 5% for breakages. This is especially important if any are to be cut.*

Laying paving

Laying paving is certainly hard work, but as this step-by-step guide shows, you can achieve some wonderful results. It really isn't as daunting as you think!

1 Mark out the patio site with pegs and string, then excavate to a depth that allows for 7.5cm/3in of hard core, plus the thickness of the concrete and paving. Take care not to damage the casing of any manholes. A lot of soil will have to be removed so you may need a sizeable skip. Finally, rake to a rough level and firm the surface.

2 Get the hard core dropped as close to the working area as possible and spread it in a 7.5cm/3in layer, making sure that it's at least 15cm/6in lower than the damp proof course. It's well worth hiring a plate compactor to flatten and bind the hard core.

3 To check that the hard core is level, cut some wooden pegs and mark one of them to the depth of the paving plus concrete base. Working from the paving boundary, knock the first peg into the mark. Drive in a second peg 1.8m/6ft along the boundary. Place a level plank over the pegs and using a spirit level, tap the second peg into the ground until the level is reached.

4 Repeat this operation around the whole boundary – in a small garden, this won't take long! Connect the pegs with string to show the overall level, the string height representing the surface of the paving. A handy way of double-checking that you've got the level right if you're working next to a brick wall is to compare the line of the string with a line of mortar in the wall.

5 To create a slight slope away from the house (to allow rainwater to run off), mark some pegs 13mm/½in less than the first batch and set them along the boundary furthest from the house. Join them with string to their opposite numbers next to the house and you'll achieve a slope of around 13mm/½in. Starting at the house wall, lay the first slabs.

6 Using the string as a guide, each slab is laid on five lumps of concrete, leaving a small gap between each one for pointing (see step 8). To save money and effort, position the corner lumps of concrete so that each one will support the corner of two slabs. Tamp the slabs down, using a heavy wooden mallet or the handle of a club hammer.

7 After each slab is laid, double-check the level – you won't be able to correct mistakes once the concrete has set! The first line of slabs should be easy to check, using the wall and string as a guide. For subsequent lines, check the level by laying a plank across the slabs to a peg, using a spirit level to check that the level is correct.

8 Once all the slabs are laid, support the perimeter with planks laid on their side, and try to keep off the area for at least 24 hours. Once the concrete has set, point between the slabs with mortar using a builder's trowel. Apply the wet mortar carefully, removing any spillages as soon as possible, to prevent them from marking the slabs.

The simplest of materials can make a pleasing path, as in this curve of mellow brick.

Now add the layer of bedding sand, firming it down, and lay the blocks in your chosen pattern, starting from one corner. Complete one small section at a time, and bed it in by laying a length of timber over it and tamping down with a club hammer. Keep checking the level as you go, and when the whole area is covered, brush silver sand into the joints so that it is almost flush with the surface.

LAYING BRICKS

Bricks are laid in much the same way as pavers, within an edging, but they are normally bedded on a layer of mortar rather than sand. Space them evenly, to allow joints for mortar, by using spacers or thin strips of wood. Once laid, brush in more dry mortar, forcing it down firmly between the bricks with a thin piece of wood, to avoid any air pockets.

LAYING PAVERS

Prepare the foundation in the same way as for paving slabs, excavating to a depth that allows for the hard core, a 5cm/2in layer of sand and the depth of the pavers. Once the hard core is in place, edge the site – a solid edging is essential to keep the pavers in place because they're bound together only by sand. Part of this edging could be the wall of the house, with paving slabs or special edging strips, concreted into position, for the remaining edges.

TIPS

✔ *If you're paving close to the house or boundary but want to grow climbers and wall shrubs, leave a 45cm/18in planting gap. Similarly, a large paved area can be enlivened if you leave out an occasional slab and plant the space up.*

LAYING PATHS

When planning a path, be sure to make it a sensible width. If it's simply a cut-through for you and the wheelbarrow, you can get away with a minimum width of 60cm/2ft. But if it's a strolling path, you need 0.9-1.2m/3-4ft for two people to walk abreast without jostling.

As with patios, there's a vast choice of materials and, again, a mix of materials can look really stylish – concrete slabs with brick, for instance, or pavers with cobbles.

Construction methods, which depend on the materials you use, are covered under patio construction, but it's a good idea to lay the path in sections about 90cm/3ft long. If you're edging the path, lay one edge first, followed by the paving material and then the second edge. As each section is finished, tamp it into position and check the level.

BUILDING RAISED BEDS

Raised beds are one of the most effective ways of adding a dash of character to patios and gardens, providing an interesting change of level and a strong structural presence. They are also, in effect, very large planters, and a great way of growing any plants that would struggle in your own garden soil. If, for instance, you garden on chalk, it's impossible to grow azaleas, but they'd romp away in a raised bed filled with lime-free ericaceous compost.

They can also make gardening easier for elderly or disabled gardeners by bringing plants up to a height where they can be tended without too much bending and stretching, especially if you incorporate a wide flat edging so that any work can be done from a sitting position.

Raised beds of brick or stone always look good, especially if they echo the materials and colours used on paths and patios. Old railway sleepers are another good choice, especially for low beds. Try to get clean, oil-free timbers, but they're like gold dust and you may have to accept the more widely available type that will ooze tar in hot weather for the first few summers. They're best capped with marine ply, to keep foliage away from the tarry surface and to allow you to sit on them. For a more natural, rustic effect, use log rolls from the garden centre for a low raised bed, or make your own by sawing up treated wooden poles and hammering them firmly into position.

If the raised bed is to be of brick or walling blocks, you'll need to lay concrete foundations which should be twice the width of the walls. When building the walls, incorporate drainage holes just above ground level to enable excess water to drain away easily. The simplest way of doing this is to leave gaps by not mortaring between every third brick in the first layer. When the bed is completed, seal the inside walls with a waterproof paint such as

The white coping on this low raised bed makes a very smart finish – a crisp contrast to the less formal grouping of pots surrounded by sea-washed pebbles. A handy seat, too, so long as you limit the number of edge-trailers.

TIPS

✔ *Remember that the height of a raised bed, particularly if it is on a concrete foundation, affects the range of plants you can grow – alpines are usually quite happy in beds as low as 30cm/12in, while larger, more vigorous plants need deeper beds. The size of the beds also affects the amount of extra watering they'll need.*

Aquaseal 40, to retain moisture and prolong the life of the brickwork.

Sleepers can be laid very quickly, since their weight and stability makes foundations unnecessary. For extra strength, lay them in a staggered bond, like bricks. If they are going to be more than three courses high, secure them with steel rods passed through holes drilled vertically into the sleepers. These rods should be hammered at least 45cm/18in into the ground.

To fill the bed, first add a good drainage layer of at least 10cm/4in of stones, rubble or broken clay pots. Cover this with fine plastic mesh or a planting membrane like Plantex, to prevent the compost from clogging the drainage layer. Fill the bed with a decent soil from your own garden, or with bought-in topsoil. Alternatively, use an ericaceous compost if you want to grow acid-loving plants like azaleas, or a really sharply drained compost for alpines – a mix of 3 parts John Innes No 3 to one part coarse grit will suit them down to the ground.

Boundaries and screens

Whether it's a hedge, wall or fence, your boundary forms part of the essential structure of the garden. But it does more than that, by enclosing and providing security and shelter for you and your plants. Clothe the fences or walls with climbers or clip the hedge into a neat, formal shape and you'll have the best of both worlds, a perfect combination of function and beauty.

And within the main body of the garden, the use of arches, pergolas, arbours and screens can provide a new dimension of height and interest. Use them as focal points, visual barriers, or just somewhere to sit and contemplate life. Use them to add style. They are among the most attractive features you can add to any garden.

BOUNDARIES

When you take over a garden the boundary material is normally already in place, but if you're in the fortunate position to be able to choose, walls are by far the best – they're attractive, permanent and need little maintenance. They do, however, cost a fortune to build. Hedges aren't always the best option for really small gardens because they take up at least 60cm/2ft of valuable space and can deprive nearby plants of water and food. That's why fences are the most popular choice. Far less expensive though not as long lasting as walls, they provide an instant barrier which can quickly be softened with plants.

TIPS

✔ *If you're not sure how high a fence you need, try the landscape architect's trick. String up a rope or wire at the proposed height and hang some sheets from it. Adjust the height until it feels right.*

FENCES

Although there are other options like concrete, chain link or plastic, the most practical choice is timber, which is sold in a variety of styles and panel sizes.

- Interwoven panels are the most popular and are made from thin strips of wood woven between vertical struts. Less substantial and less efficient than other types at cutting down the noise from neighbours or passing traffic, but they are the cheapest.
- Lapboard panels, with horizontal, wavy-edged overlapping boards cost more but look better and are more solid.
- Closeboard panels are the toughest of all, and the most expensive. Made from overlapping, straight-edged vertical boards fixed to rails, they're solid, handsome and filter out the most noise.
- Trellis can be used for a boundary, but it won't give you the privacy you need unless it's very densely clothed with plants. But it can be used to add height to fences, where it makes a very attractive 'topping'.

BOUNDARIES

Erecting a fence

Although it may look complicated, putting up a fence is a relatively simple job for the average DIY enthusiast.

1 If you're starting the fence by a wall, screw in two post brackets, one at 15cm/6in, the other at 1.05m/3½ft from the ground for a 1.2m/4ft high panel like this. The brackets must be in a vertical straight line, so use a length of wood and a spirit level to mark where they should go. Drill holes into the brick and screw in using rawlplugs.

2 Put up a taut string guide along the boundary, then make the first post hole 1.8m/6ft from the wall. Dig a hole 75cm/1½ft deep and 30cm/1ft square and pack in a 15cm/6in layer of hardcore. Put the post in, lodge it in place with rubble, and check that it is upright with a spirit level. Now fix the brackets to the post.

3 Fix the panel to the wall brackets with galvanised nails, positioning it to leave a 15cm/6in gap between panel base and ground. A mistake that is often made is to erect a post by the house wall which involves additional expenditure on post and concrete, and extra time in digging a hole. Wall brackets are very much simpler and cheaper.

4 Before you fix the panel to the first post, always check that the panel is horizontal, using a spirit level. This can be a tricky operation, and rather than using a foot as an adjuster, we strongly recommend having a friend to help at this stage. Once the panel is horizontal, hold it in position by wedging bricks under the base.

5 Now nail the fence panel to the post brackets. The post shouldn't move as you are nailing because the hard core and rubble will hold it, but don't worry if it does move slightly – the levels can be checked once more before the post is finally concreted into place. Once the panel is fixed, double-check that it is horizontal.

6 Using a stout stick, firm the rubble and hard core around the post then fill with concrete almost to the top of the hole, sloping the surface away from the post to prevent water gathering against the wood and rotting it. Leave the concrete to set overnight, and provide temporary supports to the posts if the weather is likely to turn windy. These braces can be removed as soon as the concrete has hardened. To fill in the gap that is left between the panel and the ground, use gravel boards (see right for details).

BUYING TIPS

✔ *When buying wooden fence panels, make sure they have been treated with wood preservative and are held together with rust-proof staples or nails. Fence posts should be made of hardwood or pressure treated softwood and should be guaranteed against rot for at least ten years.*

✔ *As a finishing touch, top the fence posts with post caps. They are an attractive way of improving the look of fence posts and an added insurance against weather damage. The grain end of the wood is always the most vulnerable to rotting, even when treated with preservative, and the fence posts will shed the rain and prolong the post's life.*

Fence posts are generally made from wood, although concrete posts are available (at a much higher price), which will last indefinitely and are pre-slotted so that fence panels fit in without any extra fixings. Wooden fence posts are sold in two thicknesses with the 7.5 x 7.5cm/3 x 3in posts best for fences up to 1.2m/4ft high, while the sturdier 10 x 10cm/4 x 4in posts should be used for anything taller.

The height of the posts depends on the fixing method. If you're going to concrete them into the ground, allow for an extra 60cm/2ft. In firm (but not stony) ground it's much simpler and quicker to use metal post supports, into which the post is slotted and held clear of the soil. In this instance, therefore, you should buy posts the same height as the fence.

Metal post supports with 60cm/2ft spikes are fine for fences up to 1.2m/4ft high, and the bigger 75cm/30in spikes for anything over that. To position them, simply place a block of wood in the square cup and drive the holder into the ground. When the base of the cup is at ground level, insert the post and secure it in position.

GRAVEL BOARDS

For a long lasting job, it's well worth using gravel boards (weatherboards) at the base of the fence so that it's not in direct contact with the soil, which could rot it – indeed, some guarantees against fence rotting are invalid if you don't use them. They're sold by fencing manufacturers and are usually 30cm/12in high, so allow for this when deciding what height fence panels you need. If the colour differs from that of the fence, simply treat with tinted wood preservative.

BOUNDARIES

WAYS WITH WALLS

Building good sturdy walls is quite an art, so unless you are remarkably skilled and practical, we don't recommend you that you attempt anything more than a low wall up to 45cm/18in or so high. Don't be too ambitious with the design, either. Straight walls are hard enough, curved walls should be left to the craftsman! For step-by-step advice, consult a good DIY book.

• When choosing the building material, you don't have to have an exact match with the house wall, but it should blend in, so choose the colour and style carefully.

• High walls can be rather overpowering in a small space, so you could compromise with something slightly lower (say 1.2m/4ft high) and top it with trellis.

• When building a wall, fix vine eyes in the mortar 90cm/3ft apart and every 30cm/12in high. Once set, galvanised wire can be threaded through and used as a support for climbers and wall shrubs.

Low walls can be used to create a garden 'room'.

IVY WILL CLING

Hedera colchica 'Dentata Variegata'

A brand new fence can look awfully bleak and stark, but there's one climber that will clothe it neatly without needing any support, grows at quite a lick, and looks handsome all year round. It's our good, dependable, versatile friend – the ivy.

And what an amazing choice of leaf shape, colour and size it gives us. The enormous elephant's ears of yellow-splashed *Hedera colchica* 'Paddy's Pride', the small, prettily rounded leaves of golden *Hedera helix* 'Buttercup', the arrow shape of silver-variegated *Hedera helix* 'Glacier', the deeply slashed foliage of *Hedera helix* 'Green Ripple' that gives a lovely waterfall effect. And that's just four. Only another 260-odd to go.

All ivies will grow in sun or shade, but the gold-variegated varieties colour up best in a sunny spot, while all-gold 'Buttercup' will fade to green if it doesn't get its fair share of sunshine.

In time, you'll find that ivies grow to a quite substantial bulk, and they'll look much better if you clip them back each year in March. Take them tight back to the fence, then give them a good brush to dislodge any dead leaves. They'll soon put on fresh new growth and look much brighter and perkier. If you prune back again in July, taking out any long trailing stems and levelling off the growth at the top of the fence, visitors could be forgiven for thinking that what you have there isn't a fence at all, but a rather interesting hedge.

LIVING BOUNDARIES

The alternative to a fence or wall, of course, is a living boundary – known in the trade as a hedge.

Not all hedging plants are suitable for a small garden, where every scrap of ground is precious. Privet, for instance, is horribly greedy, so it's difficult to plant anything else close to it. Hornbeam is too wide and bulky, holly a bit too prickly in a confined space. Leyland cypress is out of the question – it grows at such a rate that the garden will be cast in perpetual gloom unless you're out there every five minutes with the stepladder and shears.

Informal hedges such as rugosa roses and escallonia, aren't really suitable either, because they take up an awful lot of room. So here's our pick of the neater hedging plants that will give you privacy, shelter, a degree of sound-proofing and a very beautiful garden backdrop. We've also listed some lower-growing hedges that can be used either as 'room dividers' in the garden, or to define the boundaries of a front garden. For each plant we indicate either the maximum height, or the range of heights within which the hedge can comfortably be kept.

❧ BEECH (Fagus sylvatica)

Beech likes to keep warm by hanging on to its dead, russet-coloured leaves through winter, and very attractive they are too. A tight, narrow hedge of anything from 1.2m/4ft to 3m/10ft, it's best in sun, and is especially useful for chalky soils. Plant 45cm/18in apart. Trim in August.

❧ LAVENDER (Lavandula)

Lovely haze of grey and blue-purple for a sunny spot. 'Hidcote' is one of the most compact, 'Twickel Purple' rather taller at 60cm/2ft or more. Plant 30cm/12in apart. Cut off the faded flowers in autumn and trim to shape in April, taking the plants back by a third to a half to prevent them from becoming leggy and woody.

❧ LONICERA NITIDA

Tiny-leaved fast growing evergreen to 1.2m/4ft. The green form tolerates some shade, but the golden 'Baggesen's Gold' colours best in sun. Plant 30cm/12in apart and clip between May and September – it's very amenable to being shaped, if you fancy a castellated or wavy-topped hedge.

❧ PRUNUS x CISTENA

A beautiful little ornamental plum that makes a strikingly colourful hedge to 1.2-1.5m/4-5ft, with bright

There's no hedging your bets with lavender – it's a winner every time, especially in a cottage garden setting.

LIVING BOUNDARIES

red young leaves maturing to copper, and white spring blossom. Grow in sun, where the colour will really blaze. Plant 45cm/18in apart and trim after flowering.

❀ PYRACANTHA

Good in sun or partial shade, pyracantha's fearsome thorns make it a useful intruder deterrent, and it's pretty nifty – it can reach 2.1m/7ft after only four years if pampered, with an ultimate height of 3m/10ft. An evergreen, it also has bright autumn berries, though inevitably there will be fewer on a trimmed plant. Good on chalky soils. Plant 60cm/2ft apart and prune at any time in spring and summer.

❀ ROSEMARY (Rosmarinus)

A lovely informal evergreen for a sunny, sheltered spot in a well-drained soil, but may not be hardy in very cold districts. The vigorous 'Miss Jessopp's Upright' will reach 1.5m/5ft, at a planting distance of 60cm/2ft. Cut back by a third after flowering.

❀ THUJA PLICATA

A neat, fast growing conifer up to a height of 3m/10ft. The leaves are fruitily aromatic, and 'Atrovirens' is a good deep green. Best kept sheltered from wind, in a sunny spot. Plant 60cm/2ft apart and trim in spring and early autumn.

❀ YEW (Taxus baccata)

The Rolls Royce of hedging plants, providing a perfect,

RENOVATION

If you've inherited a hedge that's become impossibly tall and leggy, or far too wide, have a go at rejuvenating it. Many hedging plants (including privet, lonicera, beech, hawthorn, pyracantha and holly) respond well to a hard pruning, although it's not advisable for any conifers except yew. Evergreen hedges should be tackled in April, deciduous ones in winter.

To reduce height, simply cut back to 30cm/12in below the desired height. Subsequent trimming of the top growth until it reaches the right height, will thicken it up so that you've got a full leaf cover.

To reduce width, just do the same thing, but sideways. Though if you want to keep some privacy and shelter while new growth is establishing, you can cut one side the first year, the other side the next.

dense, dark green backdrop, to a height of anything from 1.2m/4ft to 4.5m/15ft. But you must be patient, and treat it extra-well in its formative years, to speed up its snail's pace growth rate of little more than 15cm/6in a year. Plant 60cm/2ft apart and trim in summer and early autumn. Very tough, and shade-tolerant.

BUYING AND PLANTING

Garden centres stock a reasonable range of hedging plants but you'll get a much better choice (and probably a better price) from one of the mail order tree and hedge nurseries who advertise in gardening magazines.

Prepare the ground as thoroughly, and plant as carefully, as you would for any other plant (see 'Plants and Planting'). Watering is especially important in any dry spells in the first year, to avoid casualties and unsightly gaps.

TRAINING

To encourage a densely bushy habit, cut all growths back by a third after planting, and cut back any long leading shoots thereafter, until the plants have reached the desired height. It seems criminal, when you just want the darned things to get as tall as possible as quickly as possible, but this cutting back is essential for a hedge that's evenly furnished from top to bottom.

Yew takes quite a time to reach maturity but it's undoubtedly the most desirable of all hedging plants, sternly beautiful and thriving in sun or shade.

PERGOLAS, ARCHES AND ARBOURS

These are the features which designers use to transform gardens from the ordinary to the 'something special'. All of them are relatively simple to install, yet they provide a new and very welcome sense of height and structure. Cover them in honeysuckle, roses or clematis and sit back and savour.

PERGOLAS

Pergolas are used in two ways; as an adjunct to patios, to give a more intimate, enclosed atmosphere, and as plant-smothered walkways in the main body of the garden.

Wooden pergolas are the most affordable, and while you can buy timber and make up your own design, they're also available in kit form from garden centres and DIY stores. But for walkways, especially in small gardens where wood could look too dominating, metal pergolas are ideal. They're made from slim tubes of plastic coated metal, usually black – very elegant and very airy. Some garden centres stock them, and mail order suppliers advertise regularly in the gardening press.

It's worth considering the following points when choosing a pergola:

- Wooden pergolas should look and feel solid. If you're not buying a standard kit, use 10cm/4in-square posts for the uprights which will make your pergola look substantial and permanent.
- The height of the pergola is important. If you're intending to grow climbers over it to cascade down from the rafters, a height of 2.4m/8ft is best, to allow room to walk under the plants rather than brushing your head against them.
- If you're siting the pergola against a north-facing house wall, you'll want as much light as possible to reach the house windows and doors, so keep the overhead beams at least 60cm/2ft apart and use climbers that will grow no higher then the posts.
- To create shade on a hot, sunny patio, increase the number of rafters and use ornamental grapevines or the gorgeous golden hop *Humulus lupulus* 'Aureus' for quick foliage cover.
- It can be unwise to drive metal post holders straight into the ground if there is any possibility of them damaging underground services. It's safest to carefully excavate the site and concrete them in position. Flat base plate shoes can be used if you're working on a concreted area.

Roses romp along a pergola, the airiness of the flowers contrasting beautifully with the solidity of the wood.

Putting up a pergola

*This lean-to pergola was built from a widely available
kit which needed very little fine-tuning to create a
handsome garden feature.*

2 Mark and drill the wall batten and house wall,
using a spirit level to ensure the batten is
horizontal. Push the large wallplug through both
batten and house wall, then fully tighten the screw.

3 Dig holes for the metal post holders, firming them in
with hard core. Place a wooden beam across all post
holders to check levels, then concrete them in. Erect the
posts when the concrete has set.

1 First measure the site carefully. Decide what height
posts to use by measuring the height of any doors
and windows which will be under the pergola. Allow
extra post height for clearance.

4 Whether you're nailing or screwing the rafters to the
frame, always drill pilot holes to reduce the risk of
these thinner timbers splitting. Clamp them firmly in
place while working on them.

5 The kit was intended for a free-standing pergola, so you will have to cut one end of each rafter to fit the house wall, leaving the notch-in so that it can sit on and be fixed to the house wall batten.

6 Working from a secure ladder or steady steps, make sure that all rafters are running parallel to each other and at a right angle to the house wall. Use two nails to keep each joint secure.

7 For greater stability, especially if you intend to grow heavy climbers, nail in corner braces between the uprights and the rafters. Some kits include them or you may have to cut your own.

8 As a finishing touch along the front of the pergola, use ready-made panels of decorative trellis like this concave arch. A slightly cheaper alternative would be to use straight lengths of 30cm/1ft trellis.

The end result – a fine garden feature, ready to be planted up with all your favourite climbers, which can be grown in pots or in the planting holes at the base of each upright.

The construction of wooden pergolas (see pages 38 and 39) is relatively simple – it's just like putting up a series of fence posts and slotting the cross-beams and rafters on top. The metal versions are even simpler, once you've worked out how to assemble all the components. The bottom 30cm/12in or so of the structure is pushed into the ground, and concreting is only necessary in very light soils or in exposed spots.

You might, at first, be horrified at how stark a brand new pergola can look, but once the rigid outline is softened with plants, it can be one of the most strikingly attractive of all garden features.

ARCHES

Arches are normally used to straddle a path, or to provide a 'grand entrance' to another part of the garden. But in small gardens they're also extremely effective set against a wall or hedge to frame a seat, pot or statue. Again, you can buy wooden kits which are very simple to construct,

and metal arches are available in a wide range of very attractive styles.

ARBOURS

Whether wooden or metal, arbours provide a retreat – an ideal, intimate place to sit, unwind and enjoy the garden. Cover them with scented plants, and as fragrance is often at its strongest in the evening, try to position them where they'll catch the late afternoon sun – the perfect place for sipping a cheering glass after a hard day's work.

SCREENS

Wooden trellis is the simplest form of screen, and is extremely useful for hiding eyesores like dustbins and compost heaps. They can also be used to divide off one part of the garden from another, but metal arches, in a variety of decorative shapes, do the job rather more stylishly.

A metal arch smothered in Clematis montana *makes an impressive and inviting gateway to the garden beyond.*

Even the most simply constructed arbour makes a wonderful spot for relaxing and enjoying the scents and sounds of summer.

SOCIAL CLIMBERS

Climbers can (and should) be used to soften house walls and make fences do a vanishing act. That's their job. But when it comes to clothing pergolas, arches and arbours, it's playtime. There's something utterly appealing about the combination of a rigid structure and a plant that's allowed to climb through it freestyle.

Clematis and roses are essential, and if you plant them together, they make one of the loveliest pictures in all of gardening; the simple, starry faces of the clematis against the full lushness of the rose. Just think of dark velvety purple *Clematis* 'Jackmannii' teamed up with the bright pink ruffled blooms of the rose 'Bantry Bay' and you'll get the picture.

Scent is especially important for pergolas over patios, and for arbours, where you can sit quietly and relish it. Roses fit the bill, of course, and you can add in piercingly sweet honeysuckle and the rich, lush fragrance of jasmine (*Jasminum officinale*).

So far so good – four classic climbers for any garden. But there are some really exciting foliage climbers that will fling themselves up and over pergolas, or twine densely round arches, to spectacular effect. One of the most astounding is *Vitis coignetiae*, with gigantic, roughly heart-shaped green leaves, rusty red below, which blaze like a bonfire in autumn. It is, however, extremely vigorous and will need to be frequently cut back, so you might prefer another ornamental vine with much neater growth, *Vitis vinifera* 'Purpurea'. The foliage is the typical vine leaf shape, but a rich wine red, aging to deep red-purple before autumn leaf fall.

For really clean, cool colour, the golden hop *Humulus lupulus* 'Aureus' is unbeatable. Sharp green-yellow leaves, deeply lobed, that look wonderful on an arch in a sunny spot, with beer-scented hops in autumn. It dies right back to the ground in winter, but soon zooms up again the following spring.

But for a sturdy pergola that can bear its weight, wisteria is a must. The flowering period is relatively short, and the pruning routine is a pain, but those cascades of white or lilac blossom are just breathtaking.

Two sure-footed climbers in perfect harmony – roses and clematis make one of the prettiest pictures in all of gardening.

SOCIAL CLIMBERS

SUCCESS WITH WISTERIA

• Buy a grafted plant – more expensive than seed-raised, but very much quicker to come into flower.

• Steer clear of Chinese wisteria, Wisteria sinensis, which is far too rampant. The Japanese Wisteria floribunda is much more controllable, and the blue-lilac flower-chains of 'Multijuga' (often sold as 'Macrobotrys') can be as much as 90cm/3ft long.

• Secure it very firmly to the support – old, woody plants become extremely heavy.

• To prune, cut all sideshoots back to five or six buds (leaf joints) from the main stem in July, then cut them back even further to two or three buds in February.

The lawn

If you have room to incorporate a lawn, go for it
— grass is the perfect foil for surrounding plants,
a soft-landing play area for children, something
that's great to walk on, sit on or simply admire.

But in the small garden it's doubly important that you keep it looking good. A small lawn is subject to a disproportionately large amount of wear and tear, and if it becomes scruffy and neglected, it will be a horrible blot on your small landscape. So give your lawn the care it needs. Its very size dictates that you won't need to spend too much time on it, and the reward will be a glowing green centrepiece for your garden.

MAKING A NEW LAWN

The first question is: turf or seed? Turf looks good immediately, smothers any lurking weeds, and can be used soon after laying. But it's fairly hard work to lay, and is the expensive option. Seed is easier, cheaper, and you can pick the perfect mixture for your garden – but you won't be able to use the lawn for the first three months, and it needs lots of attention until established.

CHOOSING GRASS SEED

Grass seed is sold in a variety of mixes, each blended from a number of strains of grasses so that they are suitable for different purposes or situations. Some will give you a bowling green, some are best suited to light shade, others are formulated to cope with anything from normal family use to an invasion by the local football club. There are even some that incorporate grasses needing less mowing and maintenance. It's a bit like tea really – you can choose the blend that suits you best. Grass seed can be sown in spring or early autumn. We prefer autumn sowings (the end of September is ideal), so that the lawn can slowly establish over winter. Weeds are less of a problem at this time of year and autumn rains can usually be relied on to water it for you.

Good preparation is essential for a successful lawn and this soil is now in perfect condition for either seeding (above) or turfing.

Whichever you choose, grass, like any other garden plant, needs a good soil to root into, so you need to prepare the ground well. Boring work, but essential for a healthy, trouble-free lawn, so don't skimp on it.

PREPARING THE SOIL

First get rid of any existing weeds and grass. The simplest way to do this is to spray the area with a glyphosate weedkiller such as Tumbleweed which doesn't persist in the soil. Once the weeds have died off (after three or four weeks), rake them off then fork over the soil, removing any large stones. Next spread a 5-7.5cm/2-3in layer of organic matter such as well-rotted horse manure over the surface, and dig it in. If the soil is heavy and sticky, dig in generous amounts of grit too – it will work wonders for the drainage.

Now rake the soil level (checking with a plank and spirit level), and remove any remaining stones or obstinate clods. Firm it by treading it down, then rake in a general fertiliser at 70g per sq m/2oz per sq yd, leaving the top 13mm/½in loose and crumbly. The soil is now ready for turfing or sowing.

LAYING TURF

Mark out the area with string and pegs (or hosepipe for a curved lawn), then lay the first row of turf along one edge, taking care that the pieces butt together nicely. For the second row, work from a plank laid over the first row (best not to walk on turf at this stage), and offset the

MAKING A NEW LAWN

CHOOSING TURF

Basically, you get what you pay for with turf. Be wary of cheap offers in the back of the local paper; you may end up with low quality field turf, full of weed and coarse grass. It really is worth buying the specially cultivated turf which is specifically grown for gardens from the best strains of seed.

Different grades are available, and hard-wearing turf (containing a proportion of tough, broad-leaved grasses) is ideal for most lawns, and essential for anyone with young children. The finer-grassed ornamental turf won't tolerate too much wear and tear, but gives a much smoother, tighter finish – though it does need more frequent mowing to keep it in tip-top condition.

Turf can be laid at any time of year as long as the soil isn't frozen, waterlogged or bone-dry. Spring is a good time, but autumn is best of all because there's less chance of long dry spells and there's also a lot less human traffic towards the end of the year.

Once delivered, turf should be laid immediately. If this isn't possible for a day or two, stack the rolls in a shady spot and keep them moist. If the delay is likely to be anything up to four days, unroll them on delivery, grass side up, and keep lightly watered. Whenever we've had turf delivered, it has always poured with rain. This is what's meant by Sod's Law.

Turfing a lawn can be hard work, but gives an instant finish. Butt the turves together tightly, and fill any gaps with compost.

turves so that they're laid like bricks in a wall. Check the level as you go, removing or adding soil beneath individual turves as needed. Trim the edges to shape with a sharp knife or spade, using the plank as a guide for straight edges, the hosepipe for curves.

Once you've finished, sprinkle some old compost in the joints between turves to help bind them together, and firm them down with the back of a rake. Water the turf well, and keep it watered through any warm, dry spells.

A well-kept lawn, glowing with health, is the perfect foil for surrounding plantings.

WHICH LAWNMOWER?

For most small lawns (under 50 sq m/60 sq yds), an electric mower with a cutting edge of 25-30cm/10-12in, should be perfect. For a top quality lawn with a close-cut striped finish, choose a cylinder model, though they don't cope well if the ground is bumpy or uneven. On general purpose family lawns a rotary model is a safe bet, and one with a rear roller will give it that classy stripe. Small hover mowers are quick and easy too, but for a really small lawn we'd be tempted to go for a simple hand push model – they do a great job, and it's a nifty way of keeping fit.

Hover mowers are light and easy to manoeuvre, making short work of cutting a small lawn.

Ideally, keep off the grass for at least a month, while it becomes established. It is safe to mow your new lawn but don't mow any lower than 2.5cm/1in until the individual turves have knitted together.

SOWING SEED

Sow the seed on a dry day at the rate recommended on the box. For an even cover, divide the seed into two batches, sowing one lot from top to bottom, the other from left to right. Lightly rake it in, and protect with netting.

Water well, and keep watered for the next few weeks. Once it reaches 5cm/2in, mow it very lightly, setting the mower to 4cm/1½in, until it is firmly established. Annual weeds will appear but the mower will soon deal with them. Perennial weeds like dandelions are more troublesome, especially as most lawn weedkillers cannot be safely used for six months after sowing, but they can be carefully dug out or spot-weeded with weedkiller.

But, mowing and weeding apart, don't use the lawn for at least three months after sowing so that it develops a strong, well-knit root system.

MAKING THE MOST OF YOUR LAWN

As we've said already, a lawn really does need to look good in a small garden. This doesn't have to be too demanding a chore, unless you're a real perfectionist, but it does require a bit of effort.

MOWING

For a good-looking, healthy lawn, try not to let the grass grow longer than 4cm/1½in. And don't cut too close –

around 2.5cm/1in for hard wearing family lawns, 13mm/½in for a luxury lawn. Any closer than that and you risk scalping it, and bare patches are very quickly colonised by weeds or moss.

Oddly enough, frequent mowing actually makes the job easier. Each time you cut, the grass pauses to gather strength, making the growth rate rather slower. So, you can whizz over it with the mower rather than ploughing through it. Most professional green keepers at places such as golf clubs aim to cut their grass little and often, with excellent results, and it works just as well in the domestic garden.

Incidentally, you don't have to collect the clippings unless you've let the grass grow very long. Short clippings can be left on the grass, rather than collected in a grass box, and will feed the lawn to a certain extent.

EDGING

If the lawn isn't designed so that the mower can skim over the edges, you'll need to trim them. Hand shears are available, but by far the easiest way is to clip them with long-handled edging shears.

FEEDING

The last thing that most people want is to make their lawns grow any faster, but lawn fertilisers do make a tremendous difference. One feed in spring can transform the lawn from a yellowish tinge to a glowing emerald green, and a second feed in autumn will green it again, and toughen it up for winter. But be sure to apply the right feed at the right time – they are specially formulated either for spring/summer or for autumn use.

WATERING

If the lawn wasn't such an important feature in a small garden, we'd simply say `don't bother' and blithely move on to the next topic. Lawns can survive even the worst drought, turning dry and crispy but perking up again the minute it starts to rain.

In a small garden, though, a brown lawn can be a relatively large eyesore. So (assuming there's no hosepipe ban to stop you), water twice a week through any dry spells in late spring and summer. To avoid evaporation, water in the evening, and aim to soak it really well, to 10cm/4in (see Tips). Light sprinklings are a waste of time, and can do more harm than good by encouraging roots close to the surface, where they'll scorch when it next dries out.

TROUBLE-SHOOTING

The easiest way to beat **weeds** is to get the grass to do it for you. So cut it regularly, feed twice a year, and keep it watered during dry spells. This helps develop strong, dense, healthy grass that will smother out most weeds.

More persistent weeds, like dandelions or plantains, can be carefully dug out or dispatched with a lawn touchweeder.

If weeds really are a major problem, then one or two applications of combined weedkiller and lawn fertiliser

Moss is a great coloniser of badly drained lawns, smothering out whole areas of grass.

(weed and feed) should sort them out. But don't be too puritanical about weeds. The odd patch of daisies actually adds some charm, and clover is now regarded as almost beneficial, because it stays green in drought.

Moss can be a bigger worry. Mosskiller will get rid of it, but the problem is that it tends to recolonise unless you deal with the conditions that are causing it. Poor drainage is the commonest reason, and the soil can be opened up by spiking – plunging in a fork to a depth of 10cm/4in, rocking it to and fro and repeating the process at 15cm/6in intervals. You can then brush in a lawn dressing of a 50:50 mix of sharp sand and topsoil (available at garden centres) which will help to keep the soil open and more free-draining. But if this doesn't work, you may have to resort to digging up the worst patches, adding plenty of grit and reseeding or returfing.

If **shade** is a problem, causing the grass to grow sparsely and letting in moss and weeds, then either the grass, or the plants that are casting it, will have to go, though sometimes you can get away with just trimming plants back so that they don't directly overhang the lawn. It's a labour of Hercules trying to keep a heavily shaded lawn going, and we're strong advocates of working with nature rather than fighting it.

Though it may be tempting fate to say so, **pests** like leatherjackets and **fungal diseases** such as snow mould (*Fusarium*) are unlikely to be significant problems on a small lawn. If they do crop up, ask your garden centre for advice or consult a specialist pest and disease book.

Don't worry too much about worm casts – they are a sign of a healthy lawn and are easily swept away when dry.

If a layer of dead grass clippings ('thatch') builds up on the lawn, rake it off to allow rain to penetrate more easily.

TIPS

✔ *Garden centres sell a mind-boggling range of lawn fertilisers. Liquid fertilisers give the fastest results, but are more difficult to apply easily. Granular fertilisers are easier (you can see where you've been), and many now come with their own built-in distribution systems.*

✔ *When you've got the sprinkler on, how can you tell when you've applied a sufficient depth of water? To save guessing, place a couple of jam jars either side of the lawn and when the water reaches the required level, turn the tap off.*

✔ *Whenever using an electric mower, always plug it in to a residual current device (RCD). If you were to accidentally cut through the cable, the RCD will cut the power in a fraction of a second, saving you from possible electrocution. These special adaptors can be plugged into any socket, cost around £15, and are available from most hardware and DIY stores.*

✔ *If a layer of old grass (thatch) builds up on the soil surface, it can cause rain to run off rather than penetrate. So rake it off (horrible job) with a spring tine rake. You will inevitably disturb the living grass and it'll look like a Dennis the Menace haircut for a while, but will soon recover.*

FIRST AID TREATMENTS FOR TIRED LAWNS

Whether you've just moved in and inherited a bit of a meadow, or your existing lawn, pampered though it is, has started to look a trifle careworn, there are a few simple steps you can take to revive it.

For a badly **overgrown** lawn, regular mowing down to 2.5cm/1in will soon have it under control, even though in the early stages it will look very yellow. Give it a feed, too, and it will soon be glowing with health.

Thin, patchy grass and **bald patches** can be revitalised by overseeding, any time between April and October. Rake the surface vigorously to loosen the soil, spike it with a fork and sprinkle on Growmore (70g per sq m/2oz per sq yd) followed by grass seed (35g per sq m/1oz per sq yd). Gently rake the seed in, keep well-watered and the new grass will soon fill any gaps.

Untidy edges can make the whole lawn look a mess. Really ragged edges can be re-cut, but if there are only one or two damaged sections, they're easy enough to repair. Just cut out a square of turf around each damaged piece, undercut it with a spade and turn it round. Fill in the damaged section with soil and re-seed.

REPAIRING HUMPS AND HOLLOWS

Humps and hollows are easy to deal with at any time of year except when the ground is frozen. But make sure the soil is moist, by watering beforehand if necessary – this keeps the turf pliable and prevents it from splitting or crumbling when it's folded back.

1 *Cut out an 'H' of turf around the offending hump or hollow, using a half moon edger or a sharp spade.*

2 *Manoeuvre a spade under the turf at a depth of 4cm/1½ in then peel the turf back gently, trying not to break it.*

3 *For a hump, remove excess soil. For a hollow (above) add extra soil. Replace the turf, firm down and water.*

Plants and Planting

Planting is one of the happiest and most optimistic of all gardening activities: the whippy stem that will grow into a magnificent tree, the gaunt bare-root rose that will bush out and give you years of flower and scent, the fat paper-skinned daffodil bulbs that will increase into substantial, free-flowering clumps over the years.

Magic moment. Preparing to plant, lavishing as much care and attention on the soil as you will the plant itself.

But in a small space it's especially important that your plants are healthy and happy – any that are ailing are going to be glaringly obvious. It is vital, too, that you choose plants that give real value in terms of colour, flower, leaf, texture and form; plants with a short season of interest, unless you love them truly madly deeply, are out.

Whether planting in pots or in the ground, do some background research on what will grow well in your area, and spend a few happy hours visiting nurseries, garden centres and local gardens to pick out all those plants that you'll be happy to rub shoulders with for many years to come.

VALUE-ADDED PLANTS

Be greedy, fussy and demanding when you're choosing plants. Not very nice attributes, but essential when you're working with a limited canvas. You want the very best from every single plant you buy – anything that's a dud for half the year is going to be a big gap in a small space.

Incorporate a good number of evergreens. They can be very beautiful in their own right and evergreen shrubs are a good background for summer flowers and your mainstay over winter, giving form and structure. Some hardy perennials are evergreen, too, so search them out – plants like bergenia, heuchera, some euphorbias, some ferns, lamium, saxifrages, sempervivums and alpine sedums.

Amelanchier is an ideal added-value tree, with its mass of spring blossom, summer fruits, blaze of autumn colour and attractive winter skeleton.

VALUE-ADDED PLANTS

The richly exotic flowers of Lilium *'Star Gazer'*
are matched by their intoxicating perfume.

But go easy on that other famous group of evergreens, the conifers. They're fine here and there as 'accent' plants (especially tall narrow conifers like *Taxus baccata* 'Fastigiata'). But they're such static plants, changing so little through the year, that if you plant them in herds or grow large specimens you'll soon find yourself getting bored with them. One of the joys of a garden is watching the subtle changes from season to season, year to year; with conifers, there's nothing much to watch.

Changeableness, the ability to look quite different from one season to the next, is a delightful quality in a plant. Look at *pulmonaria* (lungwort), for instance. In spring it's a small-leaved plant with pretty flowers, in summer a striking rosette of large leaves, heavily spotted and splashed with silver. Trees are especially good at this trick. Amelanchier is a perfect example; smothered in white blossom in spring, it gives a light, airy canopy in summer (and decorative fruits in a good year), spends two or three weeks in autumn expiring in a fabulous blaze of golds and reds, then settles down as an attractive silhouette through winter. Given that it grows just about anywhere, even in pots, what more could any gardener ask of a plant?

Then there's the little question of how long a plant is going to flower, and how good it looks when the flowers have gone. Because a brief period of flower is only

acceptable in a small garden if the plant has other virtues. Peonies, for instance, have only one short, fantastic burst of flower in early summer, but the remaining foliage is extremely handsome and takes on lovely autumn tints. Once-flowering roses on the other hand, however beautiful the blooms, are less than lovely for the rest of the year – that's fine in large gardens, but not so good in a small space where every plant has to earn its keep. So with roses in particular, always look for the word 'continuous' on the label as a guarantee of a good succession of flower, or at the very least the words 'recurrent' or 'repeat', which means that they'll have one good flush followed by further smaller flushes.

The other essential ingredient in a small space is scent because while in a larger garden it can be a bit elusive, smaller gardens trap scent and hold it and a warm, still summer evening can be a heady experience.

The heaviest, most sumptuous scent undoubtedly comes from some of the lilies, and *Lilium regale*, 'Star Gazer', 'Casa Blanca' and 'Golden Splendour' are just four of the many that will perfume the whole garden. Roses, too, can be wonderfully richly scented, especially the 'English' roses and the beautiful bourbons, whose flowers and scent are equally opulent.

Fresher, sweeter scents are provided by the likes of sweet peas, lavender, lily-of-the-valley, dianthus (pinks and carnations), jasmine, honeysuckle and some of the peonies. Daffodils and narcissi, too, can be beautifully sweet – if you haven't breathed in the piercing lemon fragrance of 'Baby Moon' (a small reed-leaved narcissus with a round, innocent face), you haven't lived.

Then there are the plants that can be defined as 'aromatic' rather than scented. Herbs, which give off their scented oils on hot days – though you may draw the line at the curry plant (a form of helichrysum) which can be overwhelming in a small space. The scented-leaf geraniums in all their wonderful variety of leaf-shape and scent, from cinnamon to cedar, peppermint and apple will need to be overwintered indoors, but they're lovely plants to pop into the border in summer.

Even winter can have its perfumed moments. The lily-of-the-valley fragrance of *Mahonia japonica* is something to savour on a grim January day. The viburnums are another useful group, some of them flowering as early as November. Richly scented *Viburnum farreri* produces its white, pink-tinged flowers on bare stems right through winter and into early spring, as does sweet, pink-flowered *Viburnum tinus* 'Eve Price', which is evergreen and rather more compact.

CHOOSING THE VERY BEST VARIETIES

Garden centres tend to stock a pretty standard range of plants – nothing wrong with that, but it's always nice to get something that little bit special or unusual, and even better if there's an assurance that it will do well for you. Here's how.

🛈 Go garden visiting. Best of all are the private gardens, whose owners are usually more than happy to talk about their plants, and to go into the likes and dislikes of anything that's new to you. And a great many will have plants for sale at ridiculously low prices. So buy a 'gardens open' guide and get yourself out and about, especially in the local area because if it grows for them, it should grow for you too.

🛈 If you spot a beautiful plant in a gardening book or magazine and the garden centre has never heard of it, consult *The Plant Finder*, available at libraries and all good bookshops. This lists a staggering 65,000+ plants and where to find them, and the majority of the nurseries listed have a mail order service.

🛈 In *The Plant Finder* you'll see that some plants have a trophy symbol next to them. This indicates that the plant (anything from a rare alpine to a widely grown apple) has won an Award of Garden Merit from the Royal Horticultural Society, and it's an award that takes some winning. Plants are rigorously assessed not just for their good looks, but for a sound constitution, ease of growth and resistance to pests and diseases. As well as *The Plant Finder*, more and more garden centres are indicating an AGM on their labelling and it's a sign well worth looking for if you want handsome, reliable plants.

PUTTING PLANTS IN THEIR PLACE

Once you've accumulated all your 'high value' plants, the next step is to devise a planting pattern that will show off each plant to its best advantage.

Make the most of foliage contrasts – the big bold leaves of hosta, for instance, with lacy-fronded ferns or feathery astilbe. Or spiky-leaved plants erupting behind mounds of softly rounded foliage. The magic of playing around with contrasting foliage is that each plant complements and highlights the character of the other, so that they both win out. Take into account the colour of foliage, too. Gold-variegated and silver-variegated shrubs, for example, won't rub shoulders happily, and will get on much better if a green shrub intervenes.

Flower colours are easier to put together, and there are few combinations that won't work. Even orange and pink can be persuaded to stop swearing at each other if you separate them with a bit of silver or green foliage.

THE GREAT COVER-UP – PLANTING IN PAVING

One of the prettiest ways of brightening up a patio is to pop ground-hugging plants between gaps or chinks in the paving. These gaps can be created deliberately (when laying the paving) or they can occur naturally – normally the first sign is a flush of weeds!

Aromatic, mat-forming thyme and chamomile are ideal for dry, sunny areas, and they seem to positively relish the odd trample underfoot. They're best planted in the spring, and it is important to keep them well watered in their first summer to help them get established. Other good choices would be houseleeks (*Sempervivum*) or pinks (the smaller forms of *Dianthus*), though they should be planted in less busy spots as they're not so resilient when trodden on.

Annuals will do well too. Alyssum, for instance, is gorgeous and will produce mounds of flower – and they're likely to self-seed so you'll get lots of plants next year too. Our favourite is the slightly taller Californian poppy (*Eschscholzia*) with its fern-like foliage and colourful pleated flowers. To sow, use a fork to loosen the soil, sprinkle the seeds in, firm down and water well.

In damper areas or shady spots, cushion-forming mossy saxifrage will thrive, as will the rather pretty bugle *Ajuga reptans* 'Multicolor' with its leaves patterned in dark green, pink and cream. Grow dainty heartsease pansies (*Viola tricolor*) here too – the

Viola tricolor and purple sage

miniature pansy flowers are produced from spring right through to autumn, and it's another great self-seeder.

GOING FOR GOLD

Golden-leaved plants have a delightful lightness of touch that's perfect for a small garden. All shades of gold from the freshest to the most deeply glowing are instantly cheering, and you'll find that even quite a large gold-leaved plant is not nearly so dominating as a similarly sized green-leaved one. Think of golden *Robinia pseudoacacia* 'Frisia', for instance. A similarly sized tree in deep green would be much more dominating in a small space.

One of the loveliest of tall golden shrubs for partial shade is an elder, *Sambucus racemosa* 'Plumosa Aurea'. The leaves are finely cut and feathered, and the shape is elegantly arching, to around 2.4m/8ft. You get the brightest young foliage if you cut branches back almost to the main stem in any frost-free period over winter, but then you'll miss the fluffy globes of palest gold flower which stud the stems just as the leaves are emerging. Like many things in gardening, it's a toss-up what to do for the best. Another easy-to-please shrub to light up a shady spot is the golden form of mock orange, *Philadelphus coronarius* 'Aureus', growing to a loosely bushy 1.2m/6ft. A bright yellow-gold in spring, it matures to greeny-yellow as the season progresses, and you have the bonus of the beautifully scented creamy-white flowers in June.

Moving to a sunnier position, you're probably familiar with the flowering currants which produce their red dangles of flower in spring. Worthy, easy plants, but if you want something really outstanding, track down *Ribes sanguineum* 'Brocklebankii'. Pale pink flowers and bright yellow leaves which are blackcurrant-

---

SETTLING FOR SILVER AND BRONZE

Silver-leaved plants, especially the larger ones, are wonderful for small gardens because their light tones make them somehow insubstantial. They may well block a view, but there's a feeling that they're doing it politely. Here are just a few of the all-time greats:

One of the most ghostly silvers of all is supplied by *Artemisia ludoviciana*, which will form a substantial clump of willowy leaves to 1.2m/4ft in a hot dry spot. *Pyrus salicifolia* 'Pendula', the weeping willow-leaved pear, is a wonderful specimen tree for a small space, making a beautifully neat mound (to 4.5m/15ft or so) of densely-packed silver-grey leaves. *Salix lanata*, the woolly willow, has beautiful rounded, felted leaves of clearest silver and fat yellow catkins; a shrubby little plant that never reaches more than 1.2m/4ft. And that other lovely willow that should be much more widely planted, *Salix exigua*. This is an airy, open shrub or small tree, with narrow, beautifully silky silver leaves that dance in every breeze and glint in

Pyrus salicifolia *'Pendula'*

the sun. Plant beneath it the grey-leaved, pale pink rose 'Celeste' and by June you'll think you've died and gone to heaven.

Bronzes, plums and purples are much more definite colours, and very attention-grabbing. They also look extremely attractive when several shades are grouped together – the plummy tones of one of the cut-leaved Japanese maples for instance, underplanted with dramatic red-

purple *Heuchera* 'Palace Purple' and a ground cover of creeping *Ajuga reptans* 'Atropurpurea'. These colours are great mixers and you'll find that one of the very best ways of highlighting their richness is to incorporate just a few apricot or soft yellow flowers. It will make you think of the last few rays of sun in a glorious sunset.

scented and hold their colour well through summer. And at only 90cm/3ft, one of the most compact flowering currants for a small garden.

Viburnum opulus 'Aureum' will also enjoy a sunny spot, where it keeps its soft yellow colour throughout summer; there's a tendency for it to fade to green in partial shade. It's a form of our native guelder rose, so you have the added enjoyment of fragrant white flowerheads in spring, and fat clusters of glistening red berries in autumn.

Getting right down to ground level, there's Bowles' golden grass, *Milium effusum* 'Aureum', a real beauty. It grows in sun or shade, forming cascades of soft-textured golden-yellow leaves. Once planted, you'll never be without a few spares, because it seeds itself about – those that land in the wrong spot are easy enough to pull out but it has the endearing habit of looking good wherever it turns up.

A golden glow, and a fine foliage contrast, from sturdy Hosta *'Gold Standard' and shaggy* Hakonechloa macra *'Aureola'.*

Hostas, too, come in a range of gold shades, but one of the brightest golds of all the hardy perennials is a form of meadow sweet, *Filipendula ulmaria* 'Aurea'. The foliage is a fresh golden-yellow, and you can keep it looking good by cutting off the flowerheads to encourage a new flush of bright leaves. Give it a moist soil and partial shade and it will soon make a fine clump to a height of about 45cm/18in.

By comparison with shrubs and hardy perennials, golden-leaved climbers are as rare as hens' teeth. The golden hop, *Humulus lupulus* 'Aureus' is a good bet, and *Hedera helix* 'Buttercup' is reliably all-gold in a sunny situation, but reverts to a bright apple-green in shade. There's also a striking new summer jasmine (*Jasminum officinale*) called 'Fiona Sunrise' that has lovely lemon-yellow foliage and exactly the same flower-power as its green-leaved counterpart, though the white flowers aren't so conspicuous against the foliage. The scent's just as good though!

CHOOSING THE VERY BEST VARIETIES

HARDY PERENNIAL FAVOURITES FOR SHADE

Most patios and town gardens have more than their fair share of shade from nearby buildings, and throughout the book you'll find plenty of plants recommended for shady positions, from bright azaleas to filmy ferns and bold hostas. Here we'd like to introduce you to even more of our favourites, so that you can really pack those shady borders and corners with good, easy-to-grow plants.

First the epimediums, which seem set for a great surge of popularity as more varieties are introduced, with ever bigger and better flowers. The heart-shaped leaves, often marked or tinted with bronze, form an attractive low (to 30cm/12in) ground cover, and if you pick a good variety, the May/June flowers are exquisite. Spidery, orchid-like 'Rose Queen' for instance, or the clear gold of 'Frohnleiten', which really shines out in a shady spot.

Then a real old favourite, lily-of-the-valley (*Convallaria*). Give it a cool, moist shade and it will romp away. If it finds the ground a little too dry for its liking, it has the obliging habit of going walkabout on its creeping rhizomes until it finds a moister spot.

Solomon's seal (*Polygonatum* x *hybridum*) is another white-flowered faithful that will grow anywhere (even in sun). Its special beauty lies in the way the flowers hang down along the arching stems while the leaves curve up and away from them, as if to show them off. A lovely plant that will increase into substantial clumps; the new

The exquisite symmetry of Solomon's seal.

white-striped 'Variegatum' is especially pretty.

Sticking with white for a minute, two foamflowers for you. *Tiarella cordifolia* is a vigorous plant covered in mid-green maple-like leaves with, in May and June, a froth of foaming white flowerspikes to 30cm/12in – an excellent, rapid ground cover plant. For something rather more restrained, opt for the similar but less invasive *Tiarella wherryi*. In a moist but well-drained soil, both will be entirely trouble-free.

How about a bit of blue for your shady corners? *Brunnera macrophylla* fits the bill perfectly. Its large heart-shaped leaves make excellent ground cover and, in May and June, it produces tall (to 45cm/18in) sprays of bright blue flowers that are easily mistaken for forget-me-nots. Even better, look out for 'Hadspen Cream', for the attractive cream edging to its leaves. Brunneras are splendid plants and not planted nearly so much as they deserve, so it's up to you to redress the balance.

Finally, saving the best for last, take a look at the hellebores. They'll all do well in shade, but *Helleborus foetidus* will positively love it – it's a rare British wildflower that thrives in a woodland situation. And yes, the name means 'stinking hellebore', but the pong is only noticeable if you crush the leaves. So let's ignore that one minor drawback and look at its virtues. An evergreen, the dark green shiny leaves are finely cut and produced in abundance, and from as early as February, the plant is topped by crowded clusters of globe-shaped flowers to 60cm/2ft. These are palest yellow-green, often rimmed with red-purple, making a striking contrast with the leaves and persisting well into early summer. One of the all-time greats for shade.

Helleborus foetidus, *with its cut leaves and pale green flowers, is one of the most striking hardy perennials for a shady spot.*

FOOD FROM THE SMALL GARDEN

If you think your garden is too small to fit in food crops, think again. There's nothing nicer than a crisp sun-warmed apple straight from the tree, a succulent fresh strawberry, or the tangy aroma of a ripe tomato. And they can be yours, with a little ingenuity.

SPACE-SAVING FRUIT

The trick with fitting fruit into a small garden or patio is to think vertical – that is, to look at all your options for saving ground space, whether you're growing in a border or in pots and tubs.

When it comes to fruit trees, there's nothing quite so space-saving as the columnar Ballerina and Minarette trees, which are rarely more than 30cm/12in wide. Ballerina trees offer only apples, but Minarettes are now available as apples, pears, plums, cherries and peaches. You could have a whole mixed fruit orchard which only takes up a few square metres.

Look to your walls and fences, too, for growing trained apples and pears. Both the slanting cordons and the espaliers, which fruit on ascending tiers of branches, can be trained flat against the wall, taking up barely any space at all.

Similarly, blackberries and exciting hybrid berries like tayberries and loganberries can be grown against a wall, ideally on a trellis so that you can easily tie in the vigorous new growth. Some varieties, like the smooth-stemmed blackberry 'Oregon Thornless', have the bonus of very decorative cut-leaved foliage which colours up well in autumn. And if, like Simon and Garfunkel, you like boysenberry more than any ordinary jam, now's your chance to grow your own.

You can even, in warmer parts of the country, grow dessert grapes on the pergola, choosing one of the late-ripening varieties like the delicious 'Muscat of Alexandria'.

Remember, too, when planning the trees for your garden, that standard apples have a great deal to offer. Spring blossom, a cooling summer canopy and autumn fruit – and a mature apple tree with its dark, gnarled trunk and branches is a handsome sight at any time of year. There are, of course, dwarf apples on M27 rootstock, but they need a good soil and lots of pampering to do well, and at only 1.5m/5ft or so they won't be much of a focal point. So take a look at trees grown on M26 (3m/10ft) and MM106 (3.6m/12ft) dwarfing rootstocks. Yes, you'll need another tree for pollination unless you're growing the new self-fertile

By thinking vertically, you can cram an amazing amount of food crops into even the smallest space.

'Cox's Orange Pippin', but all you have to do is choose a compatible variety from the Minarette trees and pop it into a nearby border.

Last and best, must surely be succulent strawberries. There is no need to create a special strawberry bed for them. They'll grow perfectly well (and look lovely) in pots and tubs, using multipurpose compost. Strawberry pots are good too, but you do have to be careful to water thoroughly, so that those close to the base get their fair share. Alternatively, grow strawberries in the air. They look terrific in hanging baskets, they're well away from marauding slugs, and they're not taking up one single centimetre or inch of ground. Why not try it?

SQUEEZING IN THE VEGETABLES

If you're stuck for garden space, many of the smaller vegetables are perfectly happy grown in pots and even window boxes and some, like tomatoes, are very attractive when they're cropping. But be choosy about the varieties you grow. Flavour, speed of cropping and ease of growth should be your criteria, so go for vegetables like French beans, radishes, lettuce, baby carrots, spring onions, courgettes (in large pots or growbags) and, in warmer districts, peppers and aubergines. Avoid the snail's pace vegetables– you'd be staring at a Brussels sprout plant for months before it deigned to supply you with enough for Christmas dinner.

Highly decorative vegetables can take their place in mixed borders – the likes of searingly red-stemmed ruby chard and the curious little asparagus pea, a low-growing plant with lovely maroon flowers and pods that are flanged and triangular in section; like asparagus, the flavour is delicate but delicious.

If you can possibly dedicate one small piece of ground to vegetables, give it a go. It's amazing what you can cram in and a small vegetable garden can look very attractive – there's something about neat rows of healthy crops that appeals equally to the eye and to the stomach. Jazz it up with a few pot marigolds and chive plants – both are pretty and both have flowers that can be added to salads. If you want to be really stylish, you could even edge the whole plot with dwarf box.

You need a sunny site, or one that's in sun for at least half the day. And ideally, try to create a plot that's no more than 1.2m/4ft wide. That way you can do all your planting and harvesting from the side of the bed, rather than having unused ground between rows for access. It also means that plants grow better because the soil is never compacted by your feet, you can plant as densely as you dare, and weeds will be smothered out by the crops.

You need to make sure that the soil is in exceptionally good health, so dig it over well and

Even lettuces can be decorative if you choose one of the coloured-leaf varieties like red-tinged 'Lollo Rossa'.

incorporate plenty of organic matter – well-rotted horse manure, mushroom compost, home-made compost; anything good and juicy that you can lay your hands on. A sprinkling of a general fertiliser like Growmore or blood, fish and bone when sowing or planting won't come amiss either.

Now, as with vegetables in pots, concentrate on premium varieties. Cut-and-come-again lettuce like 'Lollo Rossa', for instance, which just keeps on cropping, or the tastiest of the outdoor tomatoes, 'Sungold' and 'Gardener's Delight'. Have a bit of fun – grow purple beans, golden beetroots, red lettuce, white radish. And try some taste experiments – okra, pak choi, rocket, salsify and scorzonera.

Look out, too, for the increasing number of mini-vegetables being offered by the seedsmen; they're starting to cater for the small gardener in a big way. Tiny peppers and aubergines, mini cauliflowers, sweetcorn and cabbage, baby carrots, beetroots and parsnips, even a mini 'Iceberg' lettuce. And all of them taste just as good, if not better than the normal sized varieties.

Keep your plot fully planted and in constant production. If you're planting in rows, stagger them so that more plants can be squeezed into the space and no 'between-row' ground is lost. When you've harvested a crop, fill the vacancy immediately by sowing seed or popping in a few plants that you've been growing in pots. Intensive farming of the very nicest kind!

Non-edible hardy annuals like these vibrant California poppies (Eschscholzia) can look lovely in the vegetable plot, and their alien scent helps to deter pests.

Make room for Herbs

There's a place in every garden for herbs because not only do they smell good and taste good, they're wonderfully decorative. Even if you haven't got the space for a special herb plot, they're the sort of plants that will fit easily and handsomely into the general garden scene.

They can be used as specimen plants (clipped bays in tubs), as hedging (rosemary), and as edgings – neat bright chives and parsley are especially good at this. The creeping thymes are lovely left to wander between paving stones. And all herbs will grow well in pots and tubs.

You can even, if you have a hot dry spot, use them to create a small, gentle-toned Mediterranean garden. Rosemary, sage and thyme will love it, and you could add in a few of the medicinal herbs that enjoy the same conditions such as silvery artemisias, a haze of spiky lavender and herbaceous sages like the deliciously aromatic clary (*Salvia sclarea*, an annual). The congregation of scents, on a hot day, will be delicious.

But best of all, let them loose in the mixed border. From the most solid of shapes like sage to the wispy, filmy foliage of fennel, they're a brilliant foil for other shrubs and hardy perennials. Their quiet good looks are especially effective with the more old-fashioned, 'cottage garden' flowers. Foxgloves, pinks, day lilies (*Hemerocallis*), columbines (*Aquilegia*), poppies and peonies. And they've an incredible affinity with roses. Not the more stiffly formal hybrid teas and floribundas,

but the looser, flowing lines of the old shrub roses (and the newer English roses). Simple herbs like dill, fennel and sweet cicely, with their feathery leaves and 'cow parsley' heads of flower, are the perfect contrast for the roses' lush, heavy-headed blooms.

The herb garden can be an exceedingly beautiful place, especially if you mix in some of those valued for their aromatic and medicinal properties like French lavender (below). A more formal block planting (right) creates a patterned carpet of colour.

PLANTING PRACTICALS

Planting in pots (pages 64-5), is simplicity itself, but in the open ground you need to make sure that your soil is in tip-top condition. It may, of course, be perfectly fine. If it's crumbly, easy to dig, retains moisture in summer and doesn't get waterlogged in winter, it probably is. If existing plants grow sturdily and well, and neglected weeds romp away, it certainly is. In which case you can skip the next few paragraphs and leave the rest of us mere mortals to ponder on some of the problems soil can pose, and how to solve them – because this is the key to a successful garden. Good soil makes for good plants, growing evenly and strongly. Poor soil, for all but the least demanding plants, is anathema.

COPING WITH WHAT THE BUILDERS LEFT BEHIND

If you've moved into a brand new house, you'll probably be aghast at the state of the garden. If not, have a little dig and see what you find, because builders have a nasty habit of removing the original topsoil,

compacting the subsoil with their machinery, mixing in a generous helping of debris, then giving it a cosmetic sprinkling of good soil, like icing sugar on a rock-solid cake. Not all builders are quite so cavalier of course, but if you do end up with this worst-case scenario, you've a bit of hard work ahead of you.

First skim off the topsoil and pile it up for later use, then remove the debris (a classic case of easier said than done). Now you need to attack the subsoil, which is generally lighter in colour. To open it up, dig it over to at least a fork's depth, bashing it about until it's in reasonably small lumps. This is grim work, but if you don't do it, you'll be forever plagued with badly-drained areas where plants will struggle to grow.

Now make it a bit more fertile by mixing in the reserved topsoil, then cap the whole lot with more topsoil, which is relatively cheap if you buy it loose rather than bagged. Worms will take this soil down to deeper layers, to improve the diet of deep-rooted plants, and (if you've any strength and money left) you can encourage them in this sterling work by adding juicy organic matter such as well-rotted horse manure or mushroom compost.

Miserable, dull, muscle-aching work, all of it. But if you want that emerald lawn and those flowing, flowery borders, it's got to be done.

OPENING UP A HEAVY SOIL

A heavy clay soil is a beast to work with initially, but once improved, it's one of the finest soils of all, full of nutrients and suitable for an enormous range of plants.

To open it up, wait until it's at the half-way stage between bone-dry and soaking wet, and dig it over to at least a spade's depth. Break it up into lumps and leave them to dry out. Once dry, they're much easier to break down even further. Now add all the organic matter (mushroom compost, leafmould, any well-rotted manure) you can lay your hands on, to stop the clay particles from sticking together again. And, if the site tends to be waterlogged in winter, add plenty of gravel for drainage. Mix these with the clay and you'll find that you've got a top layer of half-way decent soil.

Whatever your soil type, rich, crumbly organic matter will work wonders. The addition of bonemeal when planting will also give plants a real boost.

In future, to improve the soil even further, mulch it each year with organic matter. The worms will take this down to lower levels for you.

BULKING UP A LIGHT SOIL

The problem with light soils (sand, chalk, silt) is that they can't hold on to the water and nutrients that most plants, especially in a densely packed garden, so desperately need.

The answer is, again, to apply that magic cure-all soil conditioner, organic matter. It's a bit like stopping up holes in a sieve, the humus-rich particles catching and retaining water and nutrients (and to a certain extent adding their own nutrients). As with clay soil, dig it in initially, then use it as an annual mulch.

SUITING THE PLANTS TO THE SOIL AND SITUATION

Most plants are pretty amenable when it comes to the type of soil they'll grow in. Roses, for instance, love a clay-based soil, but will grow equally happily in a peaty soil that's been enriched with plenty of organic matter. Others are pickier – plants such as pieris, rhododendrons and azaleas will turn up their toes if they're not in an acid, peaty soil. So always check the preferred soil in a good reference book or with the expert at your local garden centre. And remember that anything you can't grow in the garden can always be grown in a pot, using the appropriate compost – ericaceous compost for those picky pieris, for instance.

Another factor to take into account is the relative wetness or dryness of your soil – an astilbe, for example, loves to get its feet into a bit of soggyish ground, but will

Relishing their position in a well-drained sunny border, these tulips will get the summer baking they need for successful flowering next year.

frizzle in a dry soil. Then there's the great sun/shade divide. That web-footed astilbe, for instance, won't be too happy in sun, whereas a plant like rosemary will love it so long as the soil is well drained. So again, check before you buy.

It's a pain, this checking process, when all we really want to do is grab the most appealing plants at the nursery or garden centre and cram them in. But a bit of homework will save hours of tending the sick and needy, and give you a garden full of vibrant, flourishing plants. Happily, a vast range of plants will grow equally well in sun or partial shade, but some are fussier.

GETTING DOWN TO PLANTING

Take time over planting. It's not a job to rush or skimp, because if you don't make plants feel thoroughly at home from the start, they'll never flourish. It's not difficult, it just needs a little extra care:

Dig a generous planting hole, twice as wide as and a little deeper than the existing rootball of container-grown plants or the roots of bare-root plants (normally trees, hedging, fruit and roses, available in late autumn). If you haven't already improved your soil with lots of organic matter, add a generous quantity to the excavated soil.

Water container-grown plants thoroughly before planting. Bare-root plants should be kept in their wrapping up to this point, then soaked in a bucket of water for a while.

Remove container-grown plants from their pots, gently teasing out any roots that have wound their way round the inside of the pot (if you don't, they'll carry on corkscrewing and will never get a firm grip on the soil). Set them in the hole, mounding earth under them until the top of the rootball is level with the surrounding soil, spreading out the teased-out roots.

Fill in with the excavated soil, firming as you go, and water well.

Bare-root plants should be planted in the same way, using the dark soil mark as a guide to their original depth or, with roses, setting them in so that the knobbly point where stems and roots are grafted together is just below soil level. If the roots don't fit the hole, enlarge it, rather than trying to cram them in.

Stake trees in exposed positions, but don't use too tall a stake – a sturdier trunk and root system will develop if a certain amount of sway is allowed, so stake them to no more than 60cm/2ft.

Bulbs, of course, demand a slightly different planting technique. You can excavate a whole area for them, or just dig individual planting holes, putting a handful of gravel in the bottom if your soil is heavy and inclined to be wet. Planting depth is the vital factor – too shallow and they won't do well at all, so don't cheat. Bulb packets give guidelines, but the general rule of thumb is to plant the bulbs at three times their own depth; a 5cm/2in high bulb will, therefore, need a 15cm/6in hole. The ideal planting distance is a bulb's width apart.

PLANTING CONTAINER GROWN SHRUBS

1 Give the plant a thorough watering before planting. Dig a generous planting hole, adding plenty of organic matter to the excavated soil. Double-check that the hole is wide and deep enough by sitting the container inside it.

2 Gently ease the plant out of the pot and tease out any loose roots and any that are growing in circles around the rootball. Place the plant in the hole, spreading out the loose roots to encourage a wide, vigorous root system that will establish quickly.

3 Fill in around the plant with the soil mix, firming it down as you go to prevent any air pockets. Finally, firm down around the plant with your heel so that it is securely in position, and water well. Water through any dry spells in the plant's first year.

This newly planted rose needs a thorough soaking and should be kept well watered through any hot, dry spells in its first year to help it get established.

AFTERCARE

Keep plants well watered through any dry spells in their first year, to encourage a strong root system. This will then see them happily through subsequent summers, and they're unlikely to need watering again unless they're very close to walls or trees, or there's a prolonged drought.

Mulching plants with organic matter, as we mentioned earlier, keeps the soil in good condition, but it won't supply all the nutrients they need, so apply a general fertiliser (any rose or tree and shrub fertiliser is fine) in spring. Greedy plants like roses will appreciate a second application in July, to keep them blooming.

Prune trees, shrubs, roses and climbers as necessary. The technique varies from plant to plant and any good reference book will help you out. Many, of course, don't need any routine pruning at all, but in a small garden you may have to cut them back for reasons of space. So just a couple of tips. Don't prune any plant really hard unless you know it's OK to do so, and avoid pruning in late summer (August/September) – you risk encouraging new young growth which could be harmed by frost.

Once bulbs have flowered, leave the foliage to die down naturally, to bulk up the bulb for next year's flowers. Unsightly for a time, certainly, but the dying leaves are soon lost in the rush of spring growth in a densely planted garden.

Container gardening

Old boots stepping out in style with violas and purple ajugas

Some of the finest patios we've ever seen have been planted up entirely in pots, tubs and hanging baskets to give a wonderfully full, lush effect. Far from being limiting, containers can in fact be used to grow just about anything, from dainty snowdrops to quite large trees. The other bonus is that by tweaking the compost, you can provide perfect conditions for the whole gamut of plants from A for alpines to Z for zantedeschia.

They're tremendous value in small gardens, too. A cluster of planted pots always looks good, or you can use them as moveable feasts – growing lilies in a quiet corner then moving them into pride of place at flowering time, for instance. Or as summer-long spectaculars, filled with showy bedding plants. To coin a phrase, there's pots of potential.

CHOOSING YOUR CONTAINER

The natural, earthy tones of **terracotta** suit any and every plant, and blend beautifully into the garden picture, especially when the pots have aged and mellowed. Plain pots are remarkably good value, and sturdy, handsome things they are. The more ornate pots, some of which will cost you several arms and legs, make a tremendous impact, and the handmade pots are the loveliest of all. Terracotta, because it's heavy and stable, is especially useful for taller plants like lilies and (in larger pots) trees, which are vulnerable to being blown over in plastic pots. But do check that it's guaranteed against frost damage before you buy (it's worth keeping the receipt, just in case), and place it with care – pots are easily broken, so don't set them where they're likely to be knocked over.

Maximise the impact of your planted pots by setting them in groups of contrasting shape and size.

Plastic containers are inexpensive, but try to avoid buying the very cheapest – when exposed to the sun, they deteriorate relatively quickly, becoming brittle and easily broken. Green and brown are the colours to choose if you want them to fade into the background – white's awfully bright, and black absorbs a lot of heat, which can be harmful to plants' roots. Most stylish of all are the imitation terracotta pots – the quality varies, but some are really quite convincing, and because they're

CHOOSING YOUR CONTAINER

lighter than terracotta, are especially useful on balconies. Easier to move around, too.

For really large planters, it's difficult to beat **wooden half-barrels**. They look good, and wood is an excellent insulator, protecting plants' roots against extremes of heat and cold. The enormous volume of compost that they hold makes them ideal for growing larger shrubs, climbers and even decent-sized trees. To extend the life of the barrel, treat the outside once a year, using a timber preservative that isn't toxic to plants.

Glazed ceramic pots, generally imported from the Far East, are excellent value and frost-proof. Some of the patterned pots can be a bit hectic, but the plain pots are lovely, especially if you enhance their oriental look with plants like bamboo and Japanese maples.

More ephemeral containers include **fibre** pots, which don't last for more than a season or two, and **growbags**. Growbags are tremendous for growing tomatoes and other vegetables, and can also be used for strawberries, flowers and herbs. But the colour of the plastic can be pretty hectic. In the small garden, especially, it sticks out like a sore thumb, and the first manufacturer to offer bags in, say, British racing green, will corner the market. That said, they're incredibly cheap and in our experience a few trailing lobelia round the edge will soften the glare somewhat.

Window boxes are essentially just very long slim pots. Choose a good quality plastic, and if you don't like its shiny look, disguise it in a wooden outer sleeve. These can be bought from most garden centres or made, relatively simply, from marine plywood. Terracotta window boxes are available too, but be a bit wary. The walls are so thick that the smaller ones hold very little compost and will dry out incredibly quickly in hot summers.

And finally, remember that there's no need to be too conventional – virtually anything can be used as a container, from an old sink or trough planted up with a miniature landscape, to empty paint cans and old shoes. Drainage holes are essential, of course, and you may have to provide some, though kitchen colanders come thoughtfully pre-drilled.

GROWING SUCCESS

Do use a **good compost** in your pots and tubs. Don't try to skimp by using garden soil – it hasn't the right consistency and could be harbouring all sorts of pests and diseases.
Make sure you use the right formulation:

- Multipurpose or universal compost is excellent for bedding plants, vegetables, or anything that's being planted for just a few months. Or for real value, buy a growbag and use the contents to fill your pots.
- John Innes composts are best for trees, shrubs, climbers, roses and anything that's going to remain in the same container for several years. JI No.2 for younger plants, JI No.3 for anything more mature. Spring bulbs, too, will appreciate the good drainage these composts provide.
- Ericaceous compost suits all the acid-loving, lime-hating plants like rhododendrons, azaleas, camellias, magnolias and pieris.

It's also important to provide **good drainage**; plants can rot if they're left in sodden soil. Some wooden barrels are supplied without drainage holes, so you'll need to drill some – five well-spaced 13mm/¹⁄₂in holes will do the trick. Then add a layer of drainage material, to prevent compost from blocking the holes. A 13mm/¹⁄₂in layer of broken clay pots (crocks), small garden stones or gravel is ideal for smaller pots. A 5cm/2in layer is best for larger pots, while really big containers like barrels will need 7.5-15cm/3-6in of crocks, large stones or broken brick.

Planting is simplicity itself – just fill the pot with

Even florists' buckets can be galvanised into action for your plantings, but don't forget to provide drainage holes.

Colour theming can create some stunning effects, as these rich blue pots, capped with lavender pansies, demonstrate.

compost to within 2.5cm/1in of the rim, excavate planting holes, and set plants in at the same level as they were in the original pot. Firm the compost round them and water.

When it comes to looking after your planted pots, **watering** is the biggest chore. Smaller pots are the most time-consuming of all, drying out in a flash on hot days, and they may need to be watered twice a day. So a few larger containers may be a better bet than lots of small pots. In dry spells in summer, check the pots on a daily basis; in winter a weekly check should do.

Feeding is less onerous but just as important. Fresh compost has sufficient feed incorporated in it to last for five or six weeks, but after that they're entirely reliant on you – they can't send their roots searching for nutrients as they would in the garden.

Permanent plants such as shrubs and trees need just a couple of feeds with a general fertiliser in late March and again in late June. Plants that concentrate all their energies into one mad burst of flowering or cropping (summer bedding plants, tomatoes etc.) should be fed once a week with a high potash fertiliser such as liquid tomato food. Winter bedding plants won't need to be fed until the weather warms up in spring.

Deadhead regularly – all plants, but especially bedding plants, will flower more freely if you pick off faded blooms, and it helps to keep them looking neat.

Permanent plants will need **repotting** into larger containers every few years, but if this isn't possible (if the rootball is too heavy to lift, or if the plant has reached its final pot size), then skim off the top 7.5cm/3in of compost and replace it with fresh. This should, ideally, be done annually.

TIPS

✔ *The colour of brand new terracotta pots can be softened by painting them with a dilution of natural yoghurt or manure. This instant ageing treatment encourages the growth of attractive algae and lichens.*

✔ *Hanging basket brackets are available in a range of sizes to suit different diameter baskets. The more sophisticated models have pulleys or spring-loaded holders to make watering easier; you just lower the basket to waist height, water, then propel it back up again. But whatever type of bracket you buy, fix it firmly to the wall; a well-watered basket can weigh up to 11kg/25lb, so don't take any chances.*

✔ *Window boxes must be secured safely too, especially if they're above ground floor level. If you're placing a box on a window ledge, use angle brackets to fix it to the window frame or wall. Garden centres also sell brackets to hold boxes in place under sills and there's even a range which secures boxes to railings or the tops of walls.*

HANGING BASKETS

When it comes to hanging baskets, the traditional wire basket is the best of all, because the sides can be planted as well as the top to create a waterfall of colour. But smaller baskets dry out very quickly, so go for one of the larger models – a 35cm/14in basket holds a good volume of compost without being impossibly heavy. Plastic baskets are far simpler to plant (though you don't get the same lush effect), and for really low maintenance, choose a self-watering model which has a built-in reservoir that supplies water as the soil dries out.

Flower pouches and towers are another, increasingly popular, way of displaying plants on walls and they can look magnificent as long as the entire tube is kept watered, the plants at the bottom getting as much water as those at the top.

Even the simplest of plantings (here, petunias, busy lizzies and just a touch of lobelia) can be tremendously attractive.

GROWING SUCCESS

As with pots and tubs, a good compost is essential, and there are composts specially formulated for hanging baskets which will retain slightly more moisture than other types. We'd recommend them for wire baskets (which are the quickest to dry out), but in other more enclosed baskets a multipurpose compost will be fine.

Planting up a plastic hanging basket is quite straightforward, but hanging pouches need a little extra care. It's important that the compost is firmed in so no air pockets remain. After planting, water thoroughly and squeeze the bottom corners to check that sufficient water has reached the base of the pouch.

Life gets even more complicated with wire baskets. For a start they need to be lined, and while we'd always advocate moss as the most pleasant to look at until the basket is hidden by plants, fibre liners are rather better at retaining moisture. And planting up is a fiddly job, but when you see the great globe of midsummer colour, you won't regret a minute of the extra planting-up time.

Gardening on two levels – a superbly planted hanging basket holding centre stage above an equally pretty grouping of pots planted up with hydrangea and summer bedding.

Planting up a mossed wire basket

Planting up a wire basket is a little trickier than planting hanging pots and pouches, but is well worth it when you see the end result.

Aftercare? As for pots and tubs, with constant, even watering as top priority. In the heat of summer you may need to water up to twice a day, so check them regularly and, if possible, water in the evening or morning, when less moisture will be lost through evaporation.

1 Line the basket with moss and place a circle of plastic in the bottom to help retain water.

2 Mix slow release fertiliser and water storage granules with the compost.

3 Fill with compost, pressing it firmly against the sides without compacting it.

4 Make holes in the moss for the first planting layer and gently push in the rootballs.

5 Plant a middle layer and top off the basket with larger, more upright plants.

6 Fill in any gaps in the compost and water until the basket is thoroughly saturated.

PLANTING FOR YEAR ROUND STYLE

Visitors to major gardening events like the Chelsea Flower Show always flock to the outdoor display gardens, where the imaginations of landscape designers are on overtime and any amount of inspirational ideas are there for the copying. So take particular note of the clever way they use plants in containers. Not so much the eye-catching bedding plants (we'll come to them later), but the trees, shrubs and climbers. Why not try a beautifully formed Japanese acer in a glazed ceramic pot, a Rhododendron luteum lighting up a shady spot with its golden flowers and breathtaking fragrance, or a climbing rose romping away in a half-barrel.

These are the plants that give any paved area a sense of structure and style, something that bedding plants, however colourful, can never do. They lend a presence, a framework, for more transient displays. So take a leaf out of the designers' books and make sure that your terrace, patio or courtyard has its fair share of stylish permanent residents.

...WITH TREES AND SHRUBS

Starting at the top of the scale with **trees**, it's surprising what a wide range can be grown in containers, given a sufficiently large pot (half-barrel size or so). Pick a variety that has more than one season of interest – most ornamental cherries, for instance, though lovely for their brief period of flower, are dull as ditchwater for the rest of the year. And don't worry too much about height; anything listed as having an eventual height of up to 10m/40ft will be fine. This may seem alarmingly tall, but remember that the container will restrict its growth so it won't get anywhere near as large as this. Take as an example *Betula pendula* 'Youngii', a gracefully weeping birch which is listed as growing to 7.5m/25ft. In a container it's unlikely to reach more than 4.2m/14ft. So be bold in your choice of taller trees – the 'bonsai' effect will cut them down to size.

Smaller trees, of course, are naturals for large pots and tubs and of the many weeping varieties, *Salix caprea* 'Kilmarnock' is a real beauty. This is an umbrella-like tree with weeping branches covered, in early spring, with bright pussy willow catkins, growing to no more than 1.8m/6ft. And although it's a willow, it's perfectly happy in containers so long as it is kept well watered.

Another excellent small tree for containers is the stag's horn sumach, *Rhus typhina*, growing to 2.4m/8ft or so. It's a nightmare in the garden because it sends up

A Japanese acer in its full autumn glory, trained as a standard and relishing life in a container.

suckers (new plants from the rootstock) for miles around, but in a pot you'll be able to curb this adventurous habit. And it's one of the most elegant of trees, with a widely branching habit that has a 'Japanese garden' air to it. The ferny leaves are very attractive (especially in the cut-leaved form 'Laciniata') and give a bonfire of colour in autumn. In winter you see the reason for its common name – the shoots are thickly felted just like the velvet on immature antlers.

And for really tiny trees, try the patio plants that aren't actually trees at all, but do a very good imitation. They're usually shrubs like cotoneaster and euonymus, grafted onto a clear stem to a height of no more than 1.2m/4ft. Some are weepers, but the 'lollipop' shapes look especially good if you clip them into neat topiary globes. Just keep an eye on the knobbly graft, taking out any growth that appears below it.

Your choice of **shrubs** is almost limitless, but do try to include a good proportion of evergreens, to keep the interest going through winter. Among the finest of all evergreens are camellias, rhododendrons and Japanese azaleas – spectacular when in flower and, when they've finished showing off, they sit quietly in the background, the perfect green foil for summer flowers. They're terrific plants for shady spots, but take care to keep them well watered through late summer and autumn when the spring flowerbuds are forming.

Other bright evergreens suitable for shade are to be found in the elaeagnus and euonymus families, and you shouldn't be sniffy about laurels; they've a terrible reputation for being 'old-fashioned' but the group contains some wonderfully garden-worthy plants. One of the cherry laurels, *Prunus lusitanica* 'Variegata' makes a strikingly handsome large shrub, the glossy oval leaves edged with cream, and it lends itself well to being trained as a bushy-headed standard. Even the much-maligned spotted laurels *Aucuba japonica* can look good, especially if you use the most heavily gold-splashed of all, 'Crotonifolia'.

Then you've got the whole repertoire of deciduous shrubs: beautiful bronze *Viburnum* 'Onondaga', the fluffy pink flowerheads and lovely leaf colours of the spiraeas, the long-lasting golden display of the best form of rose of Sharon, *Hypericum* 'Hidcote'. One of the loveliest of all, though, is *Magnolia stellata*, a compact rounded shrub that is covered in large star-like fragrant flowers in early spring before the leaves emerge. It slowly reaches 1.2m/4ft and looks simply stunning in a blue-glazed oriental pot. It's equally happy in sun or partial shade, but it does prefer an ericaceous compost.

...WITH ROSES, CONIFERS AND CLIMBERS

Even if you have the smallest patio or garden, **roses** are essential because a garden isn't a garden without them. Miniature and patio roses, growing to no more than 45cm/18in, are small delights, and so uniformly compact and long-flowering that they make a tremendous impact if you plant three of the same variety in one pot. Groundcover roses are good in pots too, because you get a wonderfully draped effect around the pot, which disappears under a sea of flowers. We have a few qualms about growing hybrid teas and floribundas in pots because their growth habit is somewhat stiff and awkward, but the rounder, shrubbier English roses, with their sumptuous scented blooms, are fabulous.

For real formality, add a few **conifers** to your potted garden. They are remarkably tolerant plants, tough and undemanding as long as you don't let them get too dry, and look equally good planted solo or as the centrepiece for a mixed planting. The grey-green *Chamaecyparis lawsoniana* 'Ellwoodii' develops into a 2.1m/7ft pyramid that makes the ideal backdrop for an underplanting of bedding, bulbs and trailing ivy. In smaller pots, try *Chamaecyparis lawsoniana* 'Aurea Densa', a real beauty that slowly forms a golden-yellow rounded bush some

45cm/18in high. The narrower, almost pencil thin grey-green *Juniperus communis* 'Compressa' (45cm/18in) is the perfect choice for sink and trough gardens, and one of the very best conifers of all.

Last but by no means least, the plants that everyone looks up to; **climbers**. They are essential, especially in very small paved gardens, to give the feeling of a full-clothed leafy retreat.

The very best of all for walls is that supremely talented plant, the ivy. It's evergreen, to give you winter interest, it's amazingly varied in leaf colour and shape, and it's also very varied in size; there are ivies like *Hedera helix* 'Green Ripple' that spread to no more than 1.2m/4ft, and others, like *Hedera helix* 'Goldheart' that will form great gold-splashed sheets to 6m/20ft or more.

You'll find many more excellent climbers for walls, pergolas and pillars outlined in Boundaries and Screens and Best Climbers and Wall Plants. All will do well in large pots or half-barrels in John Innes No 2 or No 3, but do keep them well watered – these are vigorous, adventurous plants and clematis, in particular, is at risk if you let it dry out.

A luscious Fuchsia, *'Thalia' makes a lovely partner for a handsome terracotta pot.*

SPECTACULAR COLOUR FROM BEDDING PLANTS AND BULBS

Once your permanent residents, the trees, shrubs and climbers, are in place, bring on the dancing girls; the bedding plants and bulbs that will light up any paved area from early spring right through to the first frosts. Generous clumps of daffodils, densely planted tulips, pots brimming over with a mass of busy lizzies, petunias and geraniums, and those real scene-stealers, the lilies, with their magnificent trumpet flowers and heady scent.

Sounds wonderful, doesn't it? And it's one of those happy gardening games that you can play at your own speed. Starting with summer bedding, at its very simplest you can just plant up a few pots, one variety per pot, and cluster them together. Take it a stage further and you can have a go at different combinations in each pot, using two varieties in complementary colours – blue and yellow, for instance, or pink and blue. It really couldn't be easier and you'll achieve some wonderful, long-lasting effects. Once you get more experienced and more confident, you can go for the jackpot – fabulous mixes of colour, texture and form that will set

bells ringing for miles around. Thumping purples mixed with crimson, toned down by lime green; ethereal pinks and whites with palest blue; blue again, but accompanied by rich apricot and pale gold. Glorious stuff, so let your imagination run free.

With bedding plants, you have access to the riotous imaginations of the bedding plant breeders, who are a race apart. Un-named, un-honoured, they're the garden heroes of modern times. Take the **busy lizzie**, that was once a rather dull houseplant. It has been transformed into a spectacular non-stop flowering bedding plant, available in over 20 colours and as happy in sun as it is in shade. A wonderful plant for any container.

Fibrous-rooted begonias are another excellent container plant, of a similar size and similar tolerance of sun or shade, and in addition to the pretty little flowers, you get the bonus of the attractive foliage in glossy copper, green or bronze.

Petunias are rather fussier about the position they're in – if you don't give them a sunny spot they sulk and produce very few flowers. But they're wonderful plants when grown well, particularly the singles, which shrug off the wet weather that turns the double varieties to bundles of sodden rags. For hanging baskets, you can't go wrong with the 'Surfinia' forms which are astonishingly vigorous and free-flowering – to such an extent that they may need the occasional trim to keep them in their place. A good alternative in a mixed basket, where other plants can be swamped by Surfinias, is the relatively new 'Million Bells' series, smothered in beautiful tiny flowers. In smaller pots, go for the 'Fantasy' or 'Junior' petunias that only grow to half the size of the traditional bush varieties. And don't forget, when buying petunias, that the purple forms have the most heavenly scent that's as rich, dark and velvety as the flowers.

For larger containers, we love **marguerites** (Argyranthemum), which produces a constant succession of daisy flowers on well-shaped rounded bushes. Good mixers, but they look their absolute best planted alone to maximise their impact. They've evolved (another cheer for the anonymous breeders) from the simple white Paris daisy they once were to a wonderful range of gold, pink and apricot shades that include a number of very pretty double forms like the quill-petalled 'Mary Cheek'.

The sheer flower-power of bedding plants is breathtaking, swathing the garden in colour from June to the first frosts.

The two all-time favourites for containers, though, have to be **geraniums** and **fuchsias**. Taking the geraniums first, in addition to all their sterling qualities (terrific flowers, wonderful range of shapes, sizes and colours), have you noticed just how difficult it is to kill them? They're virtually gardener-proof, flowering best in sun but not objecting to a bit of shade, and barely faltering if you forget to water them now and again. A basket planted up simply with three of the open, airy continental geraniums will be an explosion of summer-long colour with an absolute minimum of care.

Fuchsias are pickier. They hate to dry out and it can take weeks before they start flowering properly again. So they're safest in partial shade, in a large pot or tub where they'll get the deep, cool root run they need. You can, of course, grow them in hanging baskets, but you really will have to be extra-zealous in your watering.

All of the foregoing are the stalwarts of the summer bedding scene, but look out for the new or improved varieties that are arriving in ever-increasing numbers. Beauties like gold-flowered bidens that just doesn't know when to stop; the blue, shooting star blooms of *Solenopsis axillaris* (also sold as laurentia and isotoma), scaevolas with their stiff, trailing stems studded with flowers that look like giant lobelias. Shopping for bedding plants is a bit like going to the January sales. It's

Something as simple as just one pot of petunias, in one colour, can light up a sunny corner of the patio.

easy to get carried away. And why not?

Don't forget that there are bedding plants to give you colour in winter and early spring, too. Try the delightful **winter pansies** and their daintier viola cousins, and the hardiest members of the primrose family, showy **polyanthus** and **'Wanda' primulas**. So don't let the pots used for summer bedding go into hibernation – keep them going through winter when any scrap of colour is a precious commodity.

By March and April, it's the spring bulbs that take over in the contained garden. Be generous with them – they're incredibly easy to grow, amazingly cheap, and range from the quietly beautiful to the truly spectacular. **Snowdrops**, **species crocus** and dainty **reticulata irises** give us the first inkling of spring and look lovely massed in individual pots, especially if you can place them on a garden table or low wall to bring them closer to eye level.

A little later, **daffodils** bring the first (and heartily welcomed) splash of bright colour of the year. One of the very earliest is 'February Gold' which, depending on the weather and where you live, might just make it in February but is more likely to be with you in early

Crocus 'Cream Beauty' and variegated ivy provide a charming spring coiffure for a terracotta wall planter.

March. There are so many to choose from (and almost without exception, all good) that we'll just give you just four of our own favourites that we're sure you'll like: little 'Tete-a-Tete', with its golden flowers chattering away three or four to a stem; prolific 'Geranium' for its multiple heads of white, orange/red cupped flowers which are very fragrant; the poet's narcissus, 'Actaea' for its scent and its glistening white petals around a tiny red-rimmed cup that gives it its other common name of 'pheasant's eye', and lastly, a quite enchanting daffodil – 'Thalia'. The sweetly scented milky-white flowers, held in twos and threes, have an exquisite poise and grace. The starry petals sweep back from the gently rounded trumpet, and the overall effect is of hovering white doves. No, we're not going over the top. You'll be as awe-struck as we are when you see it.

Tulips, too, can make their first appearance as early as March, with some lovely low-growing greigii and kaufmanniana hybrids that are perfect for smaller pots and window boxes. Many are named after composers, so you could create your own spring symphony with 'Chopin', 'Berlioz', 'Vivaldi' and 'Johann Strauss'. For larger pots, in a sheltered spot where they won't be blown about, try some of the taller varieties that can be in bloom as late as May. Beauties like pure white 'Athleet' or that other pretty white, 'Shirley', each petal delicately rimmed with a fine line of pink. Or the candyfloss pink and white 'Angelique', a tulip that's so fully petalled that it looks like a peony. Finally, to end the season with a bang, how about the astonishing

The exotic, heavily scented flowers of Lilium *regale and 'Conneticut King' soaring above the surrounding pots.*

'parrot' tulips with their enormous frilled and feathered blooms in colours from deepest purple to vanilla white streaked with raspberry sauce red.

For summer colour from bulbs, make **lilies** a priority. They look highly exotic, but are just as easy to grow as any other bulb. The starry-flowered Asiatic Hybrids such as orange 'Enchantment' and white 'Mont Blanc' are possibly the easiest of all. Well worth growing, but not scented, so if you've room for only a few lilies, go for those that will give you that rich, all-pervading perfume such as *Lilium regale* with its large waxy trumpets, pure white inside and backed with pale pink stripes. Absolutely breathtaking, and it towers above other plants at 1.2m/4ft.

To grow lilies, choose a sturdy pot at least 30cm/12in deep and 25cm/10in wide. Plant three bulbs per pot in John Innes No 2 compost and keep them well watered when they start into growth. Stake the taller varieties and after flowering, remove the spent flowerheads and feed fortnightly with liquid tomato food. They'll die down over winter, so leave them outside in a sheltered spot. The following spring, renew the top few inches of compost.

A touch of class with Topiary

A lovely way to make a grand entrance, though you'll need a good eye and a steady hand to keep these box spirals in trim.

Topiary, once the exclusive preserve of the stately home owner, with whole gardens (and whole armies of gardeners) devoted to the art, is right back in fashion – because it's absolutely perfect for patios and small gardens, fitting in beautifully with summer schemes and giving added interest and cheer in winter. From sternly formal pyramids to lollipops and (we confess a soft spot here) jolly rabbits, topiary looks wonderful and makes a striking focal point.

You can, of course, buy shaped plants such as pyramid bays and neatly clipped box balls at the garden centre, but they cost a fortune. So why not have a go at making your own. There's no great mystique about it – it's really just an extension of hedge clipping. Your creations may not be quite so perfect as professional efforts, but as you'll know if you've visited the amazing topiary garden at Levens Hall in Cumbria, even lopsided topiary has a special charm.

Small-leaved box (*Buxus*) is the easiest of all to work with. To grow it as a ball, put a young plant in a 20cm/8in pot and keep on pinching out the growing tips to encourage it to bush out. As it grows, lightly trim it to shape in spring and again in late summer. Once it has developed the desired shape and size, give it the occasional clip with shears. Any variety of box can be trained in this way, though dwarf box (*Buxus sempervirens* 'Suffruticosa') is the slowest growing.

To grow a standard 'lollipop' bay tree, pick a young plant with a single straight stem. As it grows, take out all sideshoots (but not any leaves attached to the main stem), to encourage strong upright growth. When the plant reaches 20cm/8in higher than required, pinch out the main growing tip and cut the ensuing sideshoots to three leaves. These will sprout new shoots which should also be cut back to three leaves. Keep doing this until the ball has reached the size and shape you want. From then on prune with secateurs in late spring and late summer to keep it in trim.

If you've ever fancied growing topiary animals in pots, even that's easy if you cheat and use a ready made frame. There are some glorious shapes available, from elephants to those jolly rabbits, and you can buy them at flower shows or by mail order (look in the back of the monthly gardening magazines). Box, with its small leaves, is the best plant for these more complex shapes, but for even quicker results you can use a small-leaved green ivy. Choose a pot slightly wider than the frame, position one ivy under each leg of the frame animal, and secure the frame in its early stages with small canes. As the plants grow, keep them clipped to the shape of the frame and, within a couple of years or so, you'll be trumpeting about how you once potted some elephants in your garden.

A living pun – a box box. Tremendous fun, very striking, and simplicity itself to keep clipped to shape.

Garden furnishings

The hard landscaping is done, the soil has been improved, the plants are flourishing. Time to add in the finishing touches – essential items like garden furniture – and the optional extras. These latter include features such as garden lighting, which are by no means essential but can add so much to the look of the garden (and extend the time you spend enjoying it) and sensible things like sheds, which are an option for all but the tiniest garden.

GARDEN FURNITURE

Visit any large garden centre or DIY store and you'll find it awash with garden tables, chairs and benches. To help decide what's going to be the best bet for you, ponder the following points. Do you want the furniture to be an attractive garden feature in its own right? In which case a wooden bench, for instance, would look better than a plastic seat. Do you want the furniture to be left out all year, or do you need something that will stack away into any available storage space? And (although it seems obvious) will it fit the space available? We have known people buy wonderful recliners that turned out to be too big for the patio. Finally, sit-test chairs and benches, ideally for five minutes or so, to check that they're comfortable. Some wooden benches are unlikely to pass even a two minute trial.

Plastic furniture is generally the cheapest, but the quality is variable and it can fade and become brittle in sunlight after a while, so be wary about anything at bargain basement prices.

Resin furniture is a good choice if your budget can stretch a little further. It's more solid than plastic, doesn't scratch so easily, and the colours don't fade. And it's very easy to spruce up with liquid bath cleaner when needed.

Tubular steel is another popular choice, but there's a danger that the parts can rust, so it's best stored indoors over winter.

Cast metal furniture is long-lasting and ornate, but always do the sit-test – some designs can be very uncomfortable, even when well padded with cushions. It's not particularly suitable for placing on the lawn, since they generally have narrow feet which sink in when you sit. If it is cast iron, check that the coloured coating is baked enamel – painted iron can chip and rust. Cast aluminium is cheaper, lighter and won't rust. One great thing about metal furniture is that although

A wonderful object like this peacock bench, though expensive, adds great character to the garden.

it's generally supplied in black, white or green, it's easy enough to change it to any colour under the sun by using car spray paint.

Wooden chairs, tables and benches are, we think, the handsomest of all, fitting naturally and quietly into the garden scene. The cheaper softwood furniture will rot relatively quickly unless it has been pressure impregnated with preservative, so do check before you buy, and it also needs to be given a fresh coat of preservative or micro-porous paint each year. Most softwood furniture should last for up to ten years if well cared for, but anything made from Western red cedar should do even better and last for 20 years or more.

Hardwood furniture, which is most commonly made from teak or iroko, will last for years without any treatment at all, weathering gracefully from the initial golden colour to an attractive silvery grey. If you want to restore the original colour, wash down with soapy water and stain with teak oil. If needed, a light sanding will removal any algal growth. Incidentally, do check that hardwood furniture is environmentally friendly; it should come from managed plantations where felled trees are constantly replaced.

Home-made seats, like this birch bench , have great charm – something to remember next time you're tree–pruning!

BARBECUES

There's nothing quite like a barbecue – the delicious aroma of sizzling food is, to our mind, one of the best in the world. It's also a wonderful way to entertain and a great excuse to show off the garden at the same time.

The very cheapest barbecues cost just a few pounds and are basically a lightweight container packed with charcoal. They only last for one cooking session, but they're surprisingly good – a friend of ours once cooked a three course family meal on one.

Slightly more sophisticated is a **hibachi,** a cast iron bowl with adjustable cooking racks. They're nicely compact but don't provide much cooking space, so you might be better off with the bigger brazier-type barbecue which consists of a cooking bowl on legs. The best models have a wind shield – gusts of wind blowing over the coals can double the cooking time.

Kettle barbecues have dome shaped lids which can either be used as a wind shield or fitted over the cooking area, effectively turning the barbecue into an oven, making it ideal for larger cuts of meat. They're also handy if the weather turns nasty, because the lid protects the food from the elements. Guests can be ushered indoors and all the host has to do is grab a large umbrella and rush outside now and again to check progress.

We're also huge fans of **gas** barbecues. They're clean, easy to light, you can start cooking in just a few minutes, and the heat is controllable. Basically, you get all the flavour and all the enjoyment but none of the mess and unpredictability of charcoal. They're expensive, certainly, but worth it if you're heavily into outdoor entertaining. The only problem is knowing how much gas is left, so always have a full bottle in reserve.

Another option is to build your own **brick** barbecue, using a kit bought from the garden centre. They're not difficult to construct and can make an attractive feature for the patio. But somehow we feel they're more suited to sunnier climes – there's something awfully depressing when they're stone cold and dripping with water in the depths of winter.

POTS AND ORNAMENTS

One of the quickest and certainly simplest ways of providing a focal point in the garden is to use pots or ornaments.

As we have already explored, pots can be planted, but some, like the beautifully curvaceous terracotta Ali Baba jars, look magnificent in their own right. Chimney pots, tall domed rhubarb forcers and even plain glazed pots can also be just as effective left unplanted.

Garden centres sell a reasonable range, but if you want something really striking and original, get in touch with the mail order potteries who advertise in gardening magazines. They'll supply anything from a Greek beehive jar to a barley twist chimney pot and though the best pieces are expensive, you'll have something that's beautifully crafted and highly individual.

To add a splendidly stylish touch to plain terracotta pots, you could colour-wash them with a dilute solution of water-based paint. Artistic friends of ours have found that blue/green or terracotta/pink shades are the best, but feel free to experiment – and if you don't like it, change it! Alternatively, you can decorate plain pots with pieces of ceramic or coloured glass. One of the best designs we've seen consisted of a scallop shell glued onto each face of a square terracotta pot – a simple idea, but very effective.

Pots of potential – a lick of paint, and lots of imagination, can turn a plain terracotta pot into something quite unique.

When choosing an ornament like a birdbath, sundial or statue, make sure it's going to be in scale with your garden. Ideally, it should be big enough to make a striking feature but not so large that it's overpowering. The best way to do this, rather than buying a piece on impulse from a garden centre, is to decide on the position and size by experimenting in the garden beforehand. Move an object like a stool or a chair around to give you an idea of where it will best fit in, or if you're thinking of investing in a statue, get someone to act the part for you!

And once you've got your ornament home, do make sure it's secure. Heavy items need a stable base to prevent them from toppling or being accidentally knocked over. Some ornaments are supplied in pieces for easy transport and these should be cemented together for maximum safety. The final golden rule with ornaments: don't have too many of them or the impact is lost and the garden can start to look cluttered.

OBELISKS

OBELISKS

Obelisks are a stylish way of adding height to a border. They're elegant features in their own right, and look their absolute best if you use less rampant climbers which won't entirely swamp them.

Use them singly as a punctuation point in the border, or use two, to provide balance and symmetry – one each side of a seat, for instance, or either side of a path.

The most readily available (usually by mail order through the adverts in gardening magazines) are the models made of plastic coated metal, which you can assemble in minutes. Simply make four holes in the ground, push the legs in and they're ready for planting.

You can also make your own pyramid obelisk from wood which can then be stained to the colour of your choice.

Climbing roses such as the naturally slim-growing 'Iceberg' look particularly good on the metal obelisks and are easily tied to the framework. Clematis will need additional support such as plastic netting or a spiral of twine to make an even cover.

This painted wooden obelisk adds greatly to the interest of a pretty border, and is well within the scope of a reasonably competent DIY enthusiast.

WATER FEATURES

There's something wonderfully appealing about water, whether it's still or splashing and bubbling. We think it's a highly desirable addition to any garden or patio, however small.

Ponds or pools are the first things that spring to mind when water is mentioned, and if you've room for one, go for it – the pleasure you'll get from it is enormous, and local wildlife will be deeply grateful. Think of the fun of watching tadpoles hatch, or a blackbird in a bathing frenzy. Just a few points to note:

• Site it on a level spot, away from overhanging trees whose fallen leaves could pollute the water. A sunny position is best for flowering pond plants.

• Create a pond that fits naturally into the overall design of the garden. A rectangular pond, for instance, can look decidedly odd set in an informally curved lawn. Raised ponds look particularly good in formal gardens.

• Instead of going for a preformed pond from a garden or aquatic centre, give yourself much more scope in terms of size and shape by using butyl liner.

• If you're putting fish in the pond, create one central area that's at least 60cm/2ft deep. This will remain unfrozen in even the harshest winter, protecting them and other pond life.

Even if you haven't room for a pond, there are plenty of other small water features to enjoy. One of the simplest is the barrel water garden which can be created using a half barrel (60cm/2ft across) lined with butyl or heavy duty polythene. This can be free-standing or sunk into the soil with 5cm/2in of rim above ground level. Sunken barrels look especially effective edged with cobbles and moisture-loving plants such as astilbes and hostas. In the barrel itself, grow a dwarf water lily and two or three not-too-invasive marginal plants. But fish are inadvisable, in case the barrel freezes up in winter or overheats in summer. You can now even buy new-fangled old-fashioned iron water pumps attached to wooden barrels, which cheerfully pump water into the barrel all day long with a beautiful gurgling sound.

Of course, even quite shallow ponds can be a hazard for small children, but it's easy enough to create water features that are both safe and attractive. Bubble fountains powered by a low voltage pump are the most popular and, as the pictures show on page 80, quite simple to construct. We've also spotted a slightly more sophisticated version of this idea, where a frostproof Ali Baba jar is placed on the mesh and the extension spout is pushed up through the jar. Water bubbles gently from

the neck of the jar and runs in a silky stream down the
sides – very soothing and quite hypnotic. You may have
to make a hole in the base of the Ali Baba jar (some are
unholey), or you can buy complete kits by mail order.

If space is really limited, how about a wall fountain?
Take your pick from stern lions, even sterner gods,
cheerful cherubs and grinning gargoyles, spouting water
into a raised basin or trough. Complete kits (pump and
all) are available, or consult a good water gardening
book for details of how to construct your own.

But don't forget, for safety's sake, to protect any
electrical cable by threading it through a conduit where
it runs across the garden and, if it's not a low voltage
model, plug the pump into a circuit breaker (residual
current device).

*(Right) However small your garden, you can still enjoy the
peaceful sound of trickling water, using a wooden barrel fitted
with a cast iron pump. It's a hidden electrical pump, of course,
that keeps the water flowing.*

*(Below) A bronzed sun god spouts water into an ornate
terracotta pot heaped with pebbles and planted with cushions of
mind-your-own-business (*Soleirolia*).*

Constructing a patio bubble fountain

If your patio is looking stark and featureless, give it instant sparkle by lifting a few flags and installing a bubble fountain.

1 Dig a hole large enough to take a plastic shrub tub or a dustbin cut in half. You also need to allow room for setting it in a shallow saucer-shaped depression so that water is constantly recycled back into the tub.

2 Using a butyl or heavy duty plastic liner, cut a hole over the tank and drape the liner down the sides. Place the pump on 10cm/4in of gravel, feed the cable through a conduit and connect to an earthed power supply.

3 Tuck the excess liner under the surrounding slabs, then fill the tank with water. Fit the extension pipe to the pump and cover the tank with either a perforated lid (you could use the dustbin lid) or rigid wire mesh.

4 Disguise the lid or mesh with large cobbles, then place a layer of smaller stones over the liner. Placing these on a gravel base will help prevent the shiny liner from showing through.

5 Switch on and enjoy it. But don't forget to top up the tank from time to time, especially in summer when more water will be lost through evaporation in hot weather.

GARDEN BUILDINGS

If you can squeeze one into your small garden, a **summerhouse** is a lovely addition. It's a kind of Wendy house for grown-ups, which can be a wonderfully peaceful retreat whether you're working or simply sitting and admiring the garden. Even in wet weather, there's something very relaxing about looking out over the garden while the rain thumps on the roof. Hardwood models are the most handsome, but even the cheaper softwood models can be attractive, especially if you treat them with a tinted timber preservative – green is lovely. And you can, of course, grow climbers on them so that they blend into the garden scene.

If you don't have room for a summerhouse, would a **gazebo** fit? These stylish open-sided structures, usually with a solid roof, are much less dominant than summerhouses, and look lovely with a few climbers trained up the supports. They're generally made of wood, but the lightest, airiest effect is achieved by the (roofless) metal models which are very elegant indeed.

Coming down to earth with a bump, there's the little matter of the garden **shed**. Not beautiful, and best tucked into a corner or hidden by a screen of planted trellis. But incredibly useful for storing tools, the mower, cans of paint, old bikes and all those other things you'll find a use for one day. There's a whole host of different models, and the best way to buy is to visit a show site, checking out the following points:

• Make sure that good quality materials have been used, that the timber is free from large knots (which can fall out, leaving holes) and that all the metal fittings are rustproof. If the shed is made of softwood, make sure that it has been pressure-treated with a preservative.

• It should be sturdily constructed. If it's not, it could distort over the years with irritating consequences like not being able to shut the door. To test the model you're interested in, jump up and down on the floor and lean heavily against the walls. A weak shed will flex considerably but a strongly made model will firmly resist your efforts.

Gazing out over flower-filled borders, this stylish gazebo fits very comfortably into the small garden scene.

LIGHTING

- The roof should be covered with roofing felt that has a weight of at least 20kg per 10m roll.
- The door should be wide enough to take the wheelbarrow and mower.
- At least one window will be needed if you are intending to work in it, though if you're worried about security it's probably better not to have windows at all.

There's one other functional building that you might be able to fit into your small space – a **greenhouse**. But remember that you can't just tuck them into a corner as you would a shed. They need to be in a sunny spot, ideally away from trees which may cast shade, drop dirt onto the glass or, even worse, the occasional branch. Again, it's worth visiting a show site to assess the various options and costs, but bear in mind just a couple of points: timber framed greenhouses, while the most handsome, need more upkeep than galvanised steel or aluminium; and plastic glazing, while it looks fine when it's new, can become discoloured and scratched as it ages.

LIGHTING

The joy of installing garden lighting is that it greatly extends the time you can spend in your garden, taking full advantage of long summer evenings whether you're entertaining or simply unwinding after a hard day's work. It adds a magic and a mystery to the garden, bathing the most important features in golden pools of light which contrast with the secrecy of darker areas. And, more practically, garden paths and steps can be softly lit to aid navigation in the dark.

Low voltage lights are the simplest and the safest to install, and are available in kit form. A transformer is plugged into an indoor socket (although some of the more expensive systems have outdoor transformers) and this converts mains voltage to a 12v or 24v supply to power the lights. The low voltage cable is totally weatherproof and won't give any dangerous electric

Bring the garden to life at night with a series of strategically placed lights.

Catch the glimmer and splash of a fountain at night by installing waterproof pond lights.

shocks if damaged. These kits are simplicity itself – you don't even need a screwdriver because individual lights are simply clipped on anywhere along the cable, and can be unclipped and repositioned if you need to move them. And they needn't cost the earth. A good 'starter' kit with transformer cables, four lights and programmable timer costs around £70. For the security-conscious, movement detectors, which activate the lights if there is an intruder in the garden, are a useful feature of some kits and can also be bought as add-on extras. Other kits have photocells built in, to switch the lighting on at dusk and off at dawn.

Low voltage lighting creates gentle pools of light rather than overall illumination, so if you want something more powerful, you'll need to install mains lighting. This should be done by a qualified electrician, must be connected to a residual current device (RCD), and armoured cabling should be used, buried 45cm/18in deep. Far more expensive to install, but it does have the advantage of brighter light, and you can achieve some wonderful lighting effects.

Once you've installed a system you can have great fun experimenting with various lighting methods to achieve totally different effects. For **downlighting,** mount a spotlight on a wall, tree or shed to shine down on a particular feature such as a bold planting, a handsome pot or striking statue. A single mains spotlight, strategically placed, can also be used to bathe a small patio in gentle light. Low voltage lighting isn't powerful enough to do this job effectively, but it's fine for **uplighting** – a spotlight is mounted on a spike and pushed into the ground so that it shines up into a shrub or tree. It's also useful for **backlighting,** where the light is placed behind, rather than in front of, a particular feature.

TIPS

✔ *A really subtle way of lighting ponds and other water features is to use special waterproof low voltage lights. These can be floated in the water or attached around the stem of a pump, providing soft underlighting for a fountain. Magic.*

✔ *While garden centres stock a good range of furniture, barbecues and pots, they all tend to rely on the same group of major manufacturers. But if you visit one of the bigger flower shows, like Hampton Court, you'll find a much wider and more exciting range from the more specialist companies.*

✔ *For an instant arbour or open-roofed gazebo, by far the cheapest option is to simply use two metal hoops at right angles to each other. Once the plants have grown up it, it will look almost as good as the much more expensive purpose-made gazebos.*

✔ *Ponds can be very dangerous for young children, so to protect your own children or any who visit regularly, cover the pond with a stout wire grid. Alternatively, it might be worth turning it into a sand pit for a few years!*

Making life easier

When you're creating your garden, bear in mind that while gardening is one of the finest activities in the world, sitting in a deck chair and admiring your handiwork is even better. You deserve time to relax and to enjoy it. So unless you're a fanatical weeder, tweaker and fiddler, it's good to have a garden that, as far as possible, looks after itself.

There are no real tricks; it's simply a matter of planning ahead, so that you can minimise chores like weeding, watering and mowing. The aim of this chapter is to give you time for much more important tasks like picking roses, sniffing the honeysuckle and working out how to put your deck chair up in the first place.

LOW MAINTENANCE DESIGN

Throughout the book, we've stressed that simplicity is the key to good design, and it's even more important if you want to minimise maintenance. The more complicated the shape and features, the more difficult the garden will be to look after.

It's worth considering some dramatic changes at the outset. Do you really need a lawn, for instance? Or might you be better off replacing all or part of it with paving? If you have lots of small separate flower beds, would they be better consolidated into one long sweeping border? Are there plants that are struggling in one particular area, or are taking too much time to care for? Should you replace them with something more suited to the position, or something less labour intensive?

Take a long hard look at the garden, and make a list of any features that are overly time consuming. Unless you're ridiculously fond of them, harden your heart. You'll be much better off changing them, or scrapping them altogether.

LOW MAINTENANCE PLANTS

Some plants need far more time lavished on them than others. The worst offenders are bedding plants which, research has shown, require six times more work than shrubs and ground cover plants.

So, in a labour saving garden, it makes sense to limit the number of bedding plants and replace them with something far less demanding. If, like us, you're really fond of them, just grow a few in pots or in clumps in the border – they'll still need cosseting, but the work involved won't be too time consuming.

In a small garden, every plant has to earn its keep, so pick them with care. When choosing shrubs, look for evergreens that will provide year-round structure, for plants that flower over a long period, and for varieties that need very little pruning.

Be choosy about climbing plants too. Varieties like Russian vine (*Polygonum baldschuanicum*, recently renamed *Fallopia baldschuanicum*) and *Clematis montana* are so vigorous that you'll be forever hacking them back. So always check the ultimate height. And it's worth bearing in mind that many climbers need to be tied to a support, whereas others are self-clinging and will happily do the work for you.

As for roses, some need pampering, while others are

Cut out edge trimming by surrounding the lawn with paving so that you can skim over the edge with the mower.

Easy-grow plants

Our 'best plants' sections feature all our favourites for patios and small gardens, but here we'd like to give you a round-up of the plants that we reckon are the easiest of the lot – tough, troublefree and needing an absolute minimum of attention. We've omitted trees, herbs and bulbs, because almost without exception, they're amazingly easy-going.

SHRUBS

Aucuba japonica 'Crotonifolia' (spotted laurel): evergreen with gold-speckled leaves. Will grow in sun or shade.

Berberis: deciduous or evergreen toughies that grow anywhere.

Camellia: spring-flowering evergreens for a lime-free soil.

Choisya (Mexican orange blossom): evergreen. The golden form 'Sundance' is especially colourful.

Conifers: a large range of shapes, colours and sizes. Especially useful for winter colour.

Cotinus: the purple forms are glorious.

Cotoneaster: good anywhere. Has attractive berries and many are evergreen.

Elaeagnus 'Limelight': excellent tall evergreen, yellow variegated.

Euonymus 'Emerald 'n' Gold' and 'Silver Queen': low, hummock forming evergreens.

Hebe: evergreens for sheltered positions. May need cutting back by half each spring.

Lavatera: fast-growing, very long-flowering. Prune hard each spring.

Magnolia stellata

Magnolia stellata: attractive shape with lovely scented white flowers.

Mahonia 'Charity': tall, striking evergreen with yellow flowers in winter.

Osmanthus: small, dark-leaved evergreen with scented white flowers in spring.

Pieris: lime-hating evergreen with bright red young foliage and white flowers.

Potentilla: flowers all summer. Available in a range of colours and sizes.

Photinia: evergreen with attractive, long-lasting red shoots in spring.

Rhododendrons, dwarf: lime-hating evergreens. Yakushimanum hybrids are the best all-rounders.

Spiraea: the golden foliage varieties are superb. Prune back hard each spring.

Viburnum: all are good, especially the winter flowering evergreen forms.

Yucca: spiky evergreen for sheltered spots.

CLIMBERS AND WALL PLANTS

Ceanothus: blue-flowered, evergreen wall shrubs for sunny, sheltered spots.

Clematis alpina and **C. macropetala:** bell-like flowers in early spring. No pruning needed.

Hedera (ivy): self-clinging evergreens for sun or shade.

Parthenocissus: Boston ivy and Virginia creeper are in this group of vigorous, self-clinging climbers. Will grow in sun or shade.

Pyracantha: Handsome, tough evergreen wall shrubs. Will grow in sun or shade.

ROSES *(all the following varieties are recommended for disease resistance by The Royal National Rose Society)*

Bush:
'Alexander': vermilion red.
'Elina': pale primrose yellow.
'Fellowship': bright orange, strong fragrance.
'Pink Favourite': rose pink.
'Southampton': apricot-orange.

Ground cover: (easy to prune)
'Flower Carpet': bright pink.
'Hertfordshire': carmine pink.

Achillea *'Gold Plate'*

Patio: (easy to prune)
'Baby Love': bright yellow, fragrant.
'Little Bo-Peep': miniature pale pink.
'Queen Mother': soft pink.
'Sweet Dreams': peachy-apricot.

Climbers:
'Compassion': pink and apricot
'Dublin Bay': deep red
'New Dawn': silver-pink

HARDY PERENNIALS
Achillea: long-lived flowers. No staking needed.
Alchemilla: fresh green foliage with lime-yellow flowers.
Bergenia: bold evergreen foliage with pretty spring flowers.
Campanula (bellflower): all are lovely, especially *C. persicifolia.* Taller varieties may need staking.
Crocosmia (montbretia): sword-like foliage with fiery summer flowers.
Erysimum: perennial evergreen wallflowers. Very long-flowering.
Euphorbia: striking and long-lasting display. The sap is an irritant.
Ferns: long-lived plants for shady spots.
Geraniums: most hardy geraniums have an exceptionally long flowering period.
Grasses: long season of interest. Huge variety of forms available.
Hemerocallis: arching clumps of foliage with tall lily-like flowers.
Hosta: glorious foliage, best in shade. Protect from slugs.
Leucanthemum x **superbum (Shasta daisy):** a cottage garden favourite and good for cutting.
Sedum: sun-loving, drought resistant, autumn flowering.

TIME-SAVING LAWNS

If mowing the lawn seems to be taking up an awful lot of time, it could be that a few simple changes are in order:
• The shape of the lawn makes quite a difference to the time spent mowing. Tight corners and wavy edges require a good deal of manoeuvring with the mower. So keep it simple, with straight edges, or gently sweeping curves.
• Similarly, the fewer obstacles in the lawn the better. One tree is fine, but a series of wiggly island beds will drive you mad and can easily double the mowing time. If you really love the island beds, think about incorporating them into one large bed of a simpler shape.
• Edging the lawn with bricks, pavers or paving pays off too. Set them just below the level of the lawn and you can skim over them, so that you can cut out edge trimming altogether.

as tough as old boots and need only the occasional clip with the shears. With herbaceous plants, avoid any that need staking and above all, cram in as many ground cover plants as possible – at the front of borders, around shrubs, between the roses ... anywhere. These are the real stalwarts of low maintenance gardens; ground hugging, weed smothering and, to cap it all, exceedingly attractive in their own right. Put them at the top of your shopping list.

Herbs are wonderfully undemanding but the other edibles; fruit and vegetables, can be as time consuming as bedding plants, so grow them in moderation.

Finally, whatever you are buying, make sure that it's suitable for your climate, soil and the position you want it in. If it struggles to grow, for whatever reason, it'll be far more susceptible to pests and diseases and you'll spend hours of valuable deck chair time nursing it.

MINIMISING WEEDING
Weeding is the most boring and time consuming chore of the lot. But it needn't be, especially in small gardens. By using mulches and ground cover plants, you can virtually eliminate weeds, saving hours and hours of dull, fiddly work.

The first stage in controlling weeds is to clear the garden of as much existing weed as possible. The worst offenders are perennial weeds like couch grass, brambles, ground elder and bindweed. They can be dug out, but any pieces of root that you overlook will be enough to get them sprouting up all over the place

TIME-SAVING POTS AND HANGING BASKETS

We love planted tubs and baskets – nothing can beat them for summer flower power. But what with all that watering, feeding and dead-heading, they're fearsomely labour-intensive. So don't go overboard on them if time is short, and use all the tricks you can to reduce the workload.

Watering pots and tubs is a pretty dull task, but you can save time by:

- adding water retention granules to the compost when planting up. Mix them with water, stir, and within a few minutes they swell into a frogspawn gel which you then mix into the compost. These release water as needed, and can reduce the frequency of watering by half.
- using bigger containers. The greater volume of compost means that they dry out much less quickly.
- using self-watering baskets and window boxes. They have a built-in reservoir which can hold up to a week's water at a time.
- opting out altogether and getting a drip watering system to do the job for you.

Make **feeding** simpler by mixing in slow-release fertiliser granules at planting time. They'll feed the plants for you all season long.

Your **choice of plants** can also help. Some, like fuchsias, are a nightmare if they dry out and it can take weeks of pampering to nurse them back to health. Others are far tougher and will shrug off the occasional period of neglect. Some of the best are bidens, geranium (pelargonium), begonia, busy lizzie (impatiens), petunia, verbena, helichrysum and plectranthus.

Ground-hugging Ajuga reptans *'Atropurpurea' produces attractive spikes of blue flower in June and July.*

again. So treat them with a weedkiller containing glyphosate which is harmless to humans and animals once it has dried on the plant, and doesn't persist in the soil. It's especially useful for clearing whole unplanted areas of ground, because once the weeds have died back, you can plant immediately.

The only problem with glyphosate is that it will kill anything green, so in weedy areas around existing plants, use a weedkilling gel and carefully paint it on to the weed foliage. Most weeds will succumb to the first dose but the really vigorous thugs may need several applications.

Glyphosate will also clear annual weeds such as groundsel and chickweed, but these are just as easy to remove by hand-pulling or levering them out with a trowel. It's easiest to do this when the ground is moist.

Once the ground is clean, you have a choice of weapons in the battle against weeds. If you're starting a border from scratch, the most effective and long lasting control method is to use sheets of porous planting membrane such as Plantex. Placed on the soil, it allows water and liquid feed through but suppresses weeds

A bark chip mulch looks good, deters weeds and locks in moisture so long as it is applied when the soil is damp.

A weed-beating combination of gravel and densely planted catmint, Nepeta faasenii *'Six Hills Giant'*.

entirely, for up to 20 years. Simply cut a cross through the fabric, turn back the flaps, plant, and put the flaps back in place. Finally, cover the membrane with a thin layer of chipped bark to disguise it. But do make sure the soil is in good condition before you lay it – it's going to be impossible to do anything about poor soil once the membrane and plants are in place.

Alternatively, use a loose mulch. A 7.5cm/3in layer will keep annual weeds at bay, and any perennial weeds that do make their way through can be yanked out. Chipped bark is the best of the lot and will last for three years, but it's expensive, so save it for the most

prominent areas if you're working to a tight budget. Cocoa shell looks good too, smells of chocolate, and deters slugs, but it does break down rather quickly, lasting less than a year when we tried it. Wood chips are a cheaper but less attractive option. The other great thing about mulches is that they lock moisture in; far less is lost through evaporation, so they cut down on watering too.

But before you rush out in a fit of enthusiasm to buy sackfuls of mulch, don't forget your other great allies in the weed war, ground cover plants. The prettiest, longest-lasting and most cost effective weed-beaters of all. They grow quickly and, once established, deter even the most persistent weeds. They're tough, reliable, and some will thrive in even the most awful places like dry shade under trees.

For the quickest effect, plant in groups of three, mulch around them and they'll soon be sufficiently well established to take on the weeds for you.

Among our favourites are **ajuga** (bugle), a low growing carpeter with prettily coloured foliage and **lamium**, which forms into dense mats – 'White Nancy',

Ground cover roses like bright scarlet 'Essex' are one of the prettiest of all ways of keeping weeds at bay.

Vinca minor *is a useful evergreen for colonising dry, shady places where little else would thrive.*

with its fresh white-variegated foliage is especially good. Both of these do well in sun or partial shade, as does the evergreen **vinca** (periwinkle) which creeps along the ground, rooting from runners. But go for *Vinca minor*, which has much better manners than the rampant *Vinca major*.

For taller plants, you couldn't do better than **alchemilla** (lady's mantle), with attractive scalloped leaves topped by loose sprays of sulphur yellow flowers, and **hardy geraniums** that form neat mounds, flower like mad and, many people reckon, are the finest weed beaters of them all.

For sunny spots you could also try a blue-grey haze of **catmint** (nepeta), and the remarkable **ground cover roses** which are tough, undemanding and can flower for months on end. We'd pick bright pink 'Flower Carpet', white 'Kent' or pink 'Surrey'.

MINIMISING WATERING

It always staggers us (as we stagger about with watering cans) just how much time watering can take, especially in the height of summer. Pots and hanging baskets are the most time consuming, needing daily watering in the hottest weather, but even the lawn and borders will probably need an occasional soaking.

But there are, thank goodness, ways of making life easier. The first step is to reduce the rate of water loss,

Keeping all your summer pots and tubs well watered can be quite a task, but there are plenty of ways to cut down the time you spend on them.

and bulky organic matter such as mushroom compost or well-rotted horse manure will not only perk up your soil no end, but will also help it to retain moisture. Ground cover plants and mulches also help to reduce moisture loss through evaporation, as well as keeping away the weeds that would otherwise be competing for any available water. Water retention granules can be added to the compost in pots and hanging baskets.

There are other tricks, too, like growing plants that actually prefer to be kept on the dry side. The majority of herbs, and virtually all silver-leaved plants, fall into this category. Well established trees and shrubs (anything that's been in for a year or two) can also cope without additional watering unless the drought is exceptionally prolonged.

But if watering is really getting you down, it could be worth investing in some of the latest watering devices which will do the work for you.

The neatest and most efficient way of watering a border is to use a **porous** or **'seep' hose**. When connected to a tap or even a water butt (they work on low pressure), water seeps through a series of minute holes along the length of the pipe. It can be laid on the surface of the soil and moved as required, or can be buried to a depth of 10cm/4in if it's to be a permanent fixture. Remarkably, water will seep as much as 45cm/18in either side of the pipe. Very little water is lost through evaporation and the water is targeted very efficiently at the roots of the plants. And don't think you are literally pouring money away because it's claimed that these pipes use 50% less water than sprinklers – useful if you're

Clearing away old plant debris keeps the garden looking good and helps prevent a build-up of pests and diseases.

on a meter. In hard water areas, the tiny holes can fur up over time, but a cheap magnetic descaling device fitted to the outside tap will prevent this.

Micro-sprinkler systems are always used above ground and consist of a series of small sprinklers connected by tubing. Each sprinkler produces a fine rain-like spray and the heads can be changed to provide a range of spray patterns from full to quarter circle. Again, you get targeted watering, and the pipes are unaffected by hard water and will last for years. Kits for small gardens are available, and mail order companies (advertising in gardening magazines) tend to be cheaper than garden centres.

For lawns, where you want to cover the whole area, use a **sprinkler**. A simple static sprinkler will do the job perfectly well, so don't waste your money on the grander models that are better suited to large lawns.

Pots, hanging baskets and window boxes can be efficiently watered using a **drip system**. A length of black tubing is laid around the edge of the house and a thin black tube with an adjustable dripper is connected from it to each container. The drip rate can be adjusted to suit the needs of each pot. The only disadvantage of the system is that the tubing is pretty conspicuous and can be difficult to hide unless you're very ingenious.

For the ultimate in low maintenance, get a **water computer** that you can programme to switch the water on, for a set period, at any time of day or night. Although most are battery operated, these have an irritating tendency to run out quite quickly. The best models are mains operated, connected to a low voltage solenoid

valve which is simply screwed on to the outside tap. Surprisingly, they don't cost a fortune and can come in very handy while you're away on holiday. You can even buy simple overriding devices which, if it rains a lot whilst you're off sunning yourself, can tell the computer to switch off until the soil dries out.

MINIMISING PESTS AND DISEASES

Have you read those depressing answers in the problem pages of gardening magazines which run something like 'Spray fortnightly with dioxychloromethyl from spring to midsummer'. And that's just one plant, with one 'lurgy'. What happens when you've got ten plants, all with different problems? You'd be running round like a fly with a blue posterior.

No, it's much better to take up 'preventative' gardening. Because happy, well grown plants are far less prone to pest and disease attack. So the trick is to do everything you can to help your plants thrive.

First of all, nurture your soil (see 'Plants and Planting') because the better it is, the more your plants will flourish. When buying plants, select varieties that you know will be happy in the position you've chosen; rhododendrons, for instance, will sulk in chalky soil and petunias hate shade. And before you pop them into your trolley, check them over for the slightest sign of pests or disease.

Plant them carefully and keep them well-watered until they are established. Keep an eye out for problems, because most pests and diseases are easily dealt with in the early stages. Prompt action can prevent a localised attack from turning into a major and time consuming headache.

Keep the garden tidy. Slugs and snails, in particular, hide among plant debris and old leaves, so clear old plant matter as soon as possible.

TIPS

✔ *To prevent persistent weeds such as bindweed and ground elder creeping in from next door's garden, dig a narrow trench 45cm/18in deep and line it, vertically, with polythene or planting membrane. This physical barrier will keep the weeds where they belong.*

✔ *Bark chips are expensive, especially when laid at the best weed-suppressing depth of 7.5cm/3in. A clever way to make them go three times further is to place several sheets of newspaper down first. This helps suppress the weeds and you'll only need a 2.5cm/1in layer on top.*

Top Plants

When you're gardening in a limited space, it's important that every plant earns its keep. Here's a personal selection of plants that we consider to be amongst the very best you can buy.

Best CLIMBERS and WALL PLANTS

These plants will grow equally well in containers.

❀ CEANOTHUS

Blue-flowered shrubs that love the shelter of a sunny wall. Some grow pretty wide, but both 'Burkwoodii' (bright blue) and deciduous 'Gloire de Versailles' (powder blue) have a moderate height and spread of 1.8m/6ft, with a long flowering period from midsummer onwards. These and other low growing *C.repens* are by far the best value for the small garden and can be trimmed back lightly in April to encourage tight, bushy growth.

❀ CHAENOMELES (Japanese quince)

Handsome deciduous shrubs to train against a wall – sturdy dark stems that grow at strangely 'Japanese' angles, glossy green leaves, and large waxy spring flowers followed by aromatic yellow autumn fruits (good for jams and jellies). Best in sun, on a well-drained soil. Plenty to choose from, growing to 1.8m-3m/6-10ft, in all shades from white through to deepest crimson.

❀ CLEMATIS

Superb climbers for a sunny spot, though some (asterisked below) will tolerate a north-facing position. But try to avoid the really rampant

Clematis *'Ernest Markham'*

varieties like *Clematis montana* unless your pergola's on a par with the Parthenon. What you're after, in a small space, is the longest possible season of flower, and that's provided by the large-flowered hybrids that will put on a show from June right through to September to a height of 2.4m/8ft or so. So look out for 'Comtesse de Bouchaud'*, 'Elsa Spath', 'Ernest Markham', 'Hagley Hybrid'*, 'Henryi', 'Jackmannii'*, 'Lady Northcliffe', 'Madame Edouard Andre', 'Marie Boisselot'*, 'Mrs Cholmondeley'*, 'Niobe', 'Perle d'Azur'*, and 'Rouge

Chaenomeles speciosa *'Nivalis'*

CLIMBERS AND WALL PLANTS

Lonicera periclymenum 'Graham Thomas'

Jasminum nudiflorum

Cardinal'. Happily, these are also the easy-prune varieties – just chop them right back to 45cm/18in or so in February.

Always plant clematis 10cm/4in deeper than they were in the original pot to encourage underground growth buds. If clematis wilt (a sudden collapse) strikes, these will, hopefully, be unaffected and take over. Keep the roots cool by shading with plants or paving, and give lashings of water and a monthly feed through the first summer.

❀ JASMINUM

Yellow-flowered winter jasmine (*Jasminum nudiflorum*, 3m/10ft)

looks lovely tied against a wall so that the young growths cascade forward, and it thrives even in a north-facing position. By contrast, the sweetly-scented white summer jasmine (*Jasminum officinale*) needs sun and shelter and twines vigorously to 9m/30ft. Thin out older shoots after flowering to ease any congestion.

❀ LONICERA (Honeysuckle)

Perfect for pergolas and arches, relishing the open airy conditions and a moister root-run than when grown against a wall. Happy in sun or partial shade, and best planted where the roots are shaded from hot sun (shade can be provided by other plants, or by surrounding them with paving or cobbles).

'Serotina', with large red-purple flowers from July to October, is quite a show-off. 'Graham Thomas' with white flowers aging to yellow, is quieter but equally beautiful. Look out for *Lonicera x americana* too, for its saucer-like leaves and purple-tinged yellow blooms. For a spot

Pyracantha 'Orange Glow'

that's always in partial shade, *Lonicera tragophylla* is spectacular, with masses of golden-yellow flowers. All grow to around 4.5-6m/15-20ft and all except *Lonicera tragophylla* are beautifully scented.

❀ PARTHENOCISSUS

The Virginia creepers look best in great sheets on walls and fences, rather than on arches or pergolas. Grow in sun or partial shade. All are vigorous and all are handsome, with fantastic autumn colour. One of the neatest (to 9m/30ft) is white-veined, self-clinging *Parthenocissus henryana*. If you need to restrict its growth, prune back in summer.

❀ PYRACANTHA (Firethorn)

A wall shrub of great merit for a sheltered position in sun or partial shade. Evergreen, with white spring blossom and a mass of autumn berries that persist right through winter. Of all the various forms, those two old faithfuls, 'Orange Glow' and red-berried 'Mohave' should be top of anyone's list for their consistent profusion of berries. Yellow-berried 'Soleil d'Or' is pretty, too. All grow to 2.4m/8ft or so.

Pyracantha should be tied into a framework of trellis or wire. Cut back any over-vigorous shoots and berried branches in spring. They also look good trained to a more formal shape, as an arch round a doorway for instance.

❀ ROSES

The essential climber for any garden, but in a small space it's best to get your money's worth by going for those that either flower continuously through summer, or have one main flush followed by smaller flushes of bloom. So, unless you love them deeply, once-flowering ramblers are out. For walls and pillars, the sturdy modern climbers are ideal, rarely reaching more than 3m/10ft. The silver-pink 'New Dawn', pink-apricot 'Compassion' and 'Golden Showers' (exceptionally free-flowering) are all excellent.

For a long season of flower on arches and pergolas, we'll give you just three of our favourites – 'Zephirine Drouhin' (raspberry pink), 'Madame Alfred Carriere' (white, flushed pink) and 'Gloire de Dijon' (buff yellow). All beautifully ruffled double flowers, with excellent fragrance.

When growing a rose against a wall

Parthenocissus quinquefolia

or fence, train the stems horizontally to encourage maximum flower production. Similarly, training stems around, rather than straight up a support will encourage flower formation towards the base of the rose, and will also give a good, even cover. Take out the older, woodier main stems every few years to encourage strong new stems from the base.

❀ SOLANUM CRISPUM 'GLASNEVIN'

A cheerful scrambling wall shrub with clusters of blue-purple starry flowers from June through to September, to 4.5m/15ft or more. Grow in a sunny, sheltered position and tie it into wires or trellis. To keep it neat, and within bounds, cut last season's growth back to 15cm/6in in April.

See also hedera p34, humulus p41, vitis p41 and wisteria p41.

Rosa
'*New Dawn*'

TIPS

✔ *Miniature climbing roses are ideal for patios and very small gardens, forming neat columns of colour to 1.5-2.4m/5-7ft, flowering from the end of May to the first frosts. For a wide-spreading rose, there are also rambling forms (pink 'Little Rambler' and 'Open Arms') which can be trained to a height and spread of 2.4m/7ft and, exceptionally for ramblers, will flower all summer.*

✔ *When planting against a wall, where the soil is normally very dry, try to set plants at least 45cm/18in away from it if space permits. You can also improve the soil's ability to hold moisture by digging in plenty of organic matter such as well-rotted horse manure. But you will still need to water plants through any prolonged dry spells, particularly in their first year.*

✔ *Actinidia kolomikta is a tremendously attractive climber, the leaves splashed with pink and white rather as though a careless house-painter had been at work. But it must be grown on a warm south or west wall if you want it to colour up well.*

✔ *Those climbers and wall shrubs that need a sheltered position (to give them a little extra frost protection) are best planted in spring rather than autumn. This allows them to get well established before facing their first winter in your garden.*

✔ *If, after several years, your honeysuckle grows into a hopelessly tangled mass of stems, rejuvenate it by pruning all growth back to the main stems in March.*

Best BEDDING PLANTS and BULBS

All the following grow equally well in borders and in pots and tubs.

BEDDING PLANTS

❀ BEGONIA

The fibrous rooted begonias (*Begonia semperflorens*) are the good-tempered little work-horses of the summer garden, with a continuous display of flower on compact 15cm/6in plants. Excellent in pots and boxes, or as a garden gap-filler. The taller tuberous begonias have much bigger, brighter flowers (quite dazzling in some cases) and can be stored indoors over winter. Both are good in sun or shade, and like a moist soil.

❀ BIDENS

A relative newcomer to the bedding plant scene, destined to become as indispensable as lobelia. A fast-growing trailer (to 60cm/2ft or more)

Begonia *'Treasure Trove Mixed'*

for pots and baskets, with finely cut foliage that's studded with bright yellow flowers from June to the first frosts. Easy to please, it can withstand both hot, dry conditions and a cold, wet summer. Best in sun.

❀ BUSY LIZZIE (Impatiens)

Always busy producing new flowers, on neat 25cm/10in plants. Good in sun, but superb for lighting up a shady spot. They look terrific in groups of a single colour in a bowl-shaped pot. The taller (45cm/18in) New Guinea hybrids, best in sun, have the added advantage of superb foliage colour and variegation.

❀ CINERARIA (Senecio)

Attractive silver foliage plant which mixes beautifully with other colours. Two forms are available; the feathery-leaved 'Silver Dust', growing to a small mound just 23cm/9in high, and 'Cirrus' which is double the height, with rather elegant oak-shaped leaves. Both are extremely tolerant of drought so are particularly suitable for containers.

❀ DIASCIA

Loose spikes of spurred flowers to 30cm/12in on semi-trailing stems, to give an airy, relaxed look. Wonderful in mixed plantings, because the soft salmons and apricots fit in well with so many other colours. Grow in sun, and cut out faded stems regularly for flowers from May right through to September.

❀ FUCHSIA

Essential, showy, free-flowering plants for pots and tubs in sun or partial shade. Good for hanging baskets too, but don't let them dry out – they'll need intensive care for several weeks if you do. Overwinter in a cool spot indoors, reducing

Bidens

Impatiens New Guinea hybrids

Diascia

watering until they're almost dry. When the first leaf-buds appear in spring, gradually increase watering, and cut back to shape. No particular recommendations – they're all good.

❀ GERANIUM (Pelargonium)

The other essential plant for summer pots – and what a selection! Uprights, trailers, singles, doubles, and a tremendous choice of flower colour in the white/pink/red range. They'll flower right through summer, with the exception of the 'regals' (showy flowers, saw-toothed leaves) whose main flush is in early summer. We especially like the open, starburst sprays of the 'continental' types. Grow in a sunny spot and overwinter like fuchsias or, in a warmer room, treat them as a houseplant and water more regularly.

❀ LOBELIA

A useful, frothy-flowered filler for pots or any garden soil that isn't too dry. The 'Riviera' series for compact plants in attractive shades of sky and sea blue, and the trailing 'Regatta' series, particularly 'Blue Splash', a lovely dainty white-edged sea blue. All are best in sun.

❀ MARGUERITE (Argyranthemum)

Free-flowering, nicely domed plants, from the classic white Paris daisy to some remarkable singles and doubles in shades of pink, peach and gold. For ultra-compact plants (to around 30cm/12in), look out for shell-pink 'Petite Pink' and white 'Snowflake'. Whites and yellows are best in sun, other colours, which can be bleached by strong sun, in partial shade. Overwinter in the same way as fuchsias .

'Continental' geraniums

BEDDING PLANTS

Fuchsia *'Paula Jane'*

Nicotiana *'Domino Salmon Pink'*

❀ MIMULUS
(Monkey flower)

One of the most colourful plants for shady positions, with cheery nasturtium-like flowers throughout the summer. But to do their best they need a moist soil, so aren't the easiest choice for a container. For maximum impact, try the vibrant red, orange and yellow shades, though more cautious souls, like us, find the pastel mixes particularly attractive.

❀ NICOTIANA
(Tobacco plant)

The breeders have done some lovely things with nicotianas – 'Domino Salmon Pink', for instance, is a wonderfully luminous colour – but in most cases they've omitted the vital ingredient of scent. For this you need 'Lime Green' or the 'Sensation Mixed' series, which is available in a wide colour range to 90cm/3ft. Nicotianas are equally happy in sun or partial shade.

❀ OSTEOSPERNUM

Dazzling South African daisies with

a profusion of tall-stemmed flowers from June through to September. Sun lovers, they're ideal for borders or pots. Most reach 45cm/18in, though a few more compact forms are available. Colours range from a glistening white and creamy yellow through to deep purple. A number are hardy but most are tender perennials and should be overwintered indoors.

❀ PANSY (Viola)

Especially useful for winter pots and baskets, where they'll flower pretty consistently through any warmer spells and bulk up in spring to put on a fabulous show right through to May. Plant them with tulips for a really stunning contrast. Much easier to look after than summer pansies, which suffer in hot, dry weather. Grow in sun or partial shade, and dead-head regularly.

❀ PETUNIA

Another of the breeders' favourites, in a bewildering range of colours, flower types and habits. For a

stupendous show, go for 'Surfinia' (trailing and bushing to 1.2m/4ft). For a more compact trailer, try small-flowered 'Million Bells'. 'Fantasy' petunias are useful little plants for pots and tubs, reaching no more than around 10cm/4in. Grow in sun.

❀ POLYANTHUS

One of the brightest of spring perennials, in a wide range of colours, good in containers but particularly effective *en masse* in the border. Primrose-like flowers in generous clusters atop sturdy stems throughout spring – the 'Crescendo' hybrids can be in bloom as early as January. Happy in sun or shade, but prefer a moist soil. Watch out for slugs who love them as much as we do.

❀ SOLENOPSIS
(Laurentia/Isotoma)

For a relatively new plant, it's got a surprising number of different names but don't let that put you off – this is a charmer. Forms a 23cm/9in mound of feathery foliage, smothered in dainty star-

Marguerite

Verbena

like, lightly scented flowers throughout summer. A white form is available, but it's the pinks and blues that have most impact.

❀ VERBENA

A lovely filler for a sunny spot, the trailing varieties make excellent summer ground cover or edge-breakers for raised beds, tubs and baskets. 'Tapien', in pink or violet, is especially free-flowering. Also worth tracking down is 'Pink Parfait', with a good scent and luscious flowerheads in a delightful mix of pale-, blush- and rose-pink.

BULBS

❀ ALLIUM

Upmarket onions for early summer. Best known are the 'drumstick' alliums and one of the neatest, at 45cm/18in, is *Allium christophii* with glittering heads of star-shaped violet flowers. *Allium moly* is a much more informal plant, with loose heads of bright gold stars, while *Allium cernuum* produces rounded, rose-pink flowers held in dangling clusters (both to 30cm/12in or so). Grow in sun, in well-drained soil.

❀ ANEMONE BLANDA

Hugely cheerful plants for a sunny spot, forming low mats of starry pink, white or blue flower from February to April. Especially useful as a front-of-border plant under deciduous shrubs. Don't waste them in shade – it's the sun that prompts the flowers to open.

❀ CROCUS

The fat, large-flowered 'Dutch' crocus put on a fine show, but we prefer the more refined specie

BULBS

crocus that flower between January and March. 'Cream Beauty', with its rich cream, fragrant flowers, the dramatic white and deep purple of 'Ladykiller', the fine dark striping of pale lilac 'Pickwick'. Lovely things, best in sun on a well-drained soil.

❀ CYCLAMEN

The hardy garden cyclamen (*Cyclamen coum* and *C. hederifolium/neapolitanum*) are the best possible plants for impossible places, growing even in the dry soil found under hedges and trees. Flowering through winter in all shades from magenta to white against prettily marbled leaves, they'll produce more and more flowers as the tubers age, and self-seed into quite a colony. Most easily established from pot-grown plants rather than dried corms.

❀ DAFFODIL (Narcissus)

Spring hasn't sprung until the daffodils appear, and it's the dwarf and specie narcissi that look best in a small garden. Long-trumpeted 'Jumblie'; dainty-flowered 'Baby Moon' and 'Hawera'; exquisite

Allium cernuum

'Pipit', the creamy white of the trumpets shading through to lemon-yellow petals. Plant lots, in clumps, in sun or partial shade.

❀ IRIS RETICULATA

Delightful flowers for January and February, in a sunny position on well-drained soil, to no more than 12.5cm/5in. Take 'Joyce' as an example – a velvet texture, good scent, and the blue of a hot summer sky, the lower petals painted with feathery white around a deep gold stripe. An exquisite starting point for a collection.

❀ LILY (Lilium)

Yes, we admit, they're mostly pretty tall, and yes, the flowering period is short. But they are so beautiful that we can't imagine gardening without them. Two of our favourites are the white form of the turk's cap lily, *Lilium martagon* var. *album*, with airy spikes of fully reflexed flowers, and the sumptuously-scented *Lilium regale*, with its huge waxy

Crocus *'Lady Killer'*

Narcissus *'Pipit'*

white trumpets backed in wine purple. Both grow to around 1.2m/4ftin sun or partial shade and need a well-drained soil and protection from slugs.

❀ TULIPS

Wonderful bulbs for showy spring colour, but tricky to keep going unless you lift and store them each year. That's a chore, so your best bet is to go for the more tolerant types that are closer to their wild ancestors. The kaufmanniana hybrids are cheery little things, rarely exceeding 25cm/10in and often sporting maroon-striped leaves. *Tulipa tarda* and *Tulipa turkestanica* (15cm/6in) have starry flowers in white and gold, several to a stem. All tulips are best in well-drained soil in a spot where the bulbs will be baked by summer sun.

Lilium martagon *'Album'*

Tulipa tarda

Galanthus 'S. *Arnott*'

TIPS

✔ *Several nurseries and seedsmen now issue mail order catalogues of young bedding plants at various stages of growth. We've always found them good value, good quality and beautifully packed – and it greatly extends your choice of varieties since they supply a much wider range than the average garden centre.*

✔ *Most gardeners are familiar with cheerful little blue-flowered* Muscari armeniacum, *an April/May flowering bulb. But the much more unusual* Muscari latifolium *is well worth looking out for. The leaves are wider, and the flowerspikes bi-coloured – deep purple at the base of the spike, sky blue at the top. Lovely planted with two-tone blue pansies.*

✔ *Snowdrops (*Galanthus*), with the wonderful country name of 'fair maids of February', are highly prized for their appearance so early in the year. But the dried bulbs can be difficult to establish, so try to buy them 'in the green', i.e. just after flowering, and plant them at the same depth as they were originally. Water them in well and they'll barely know they've moved.*

SHRUBS

Best SMALL PLANTS

All of these plants will grow equally well in pots and tubs.

SHRUBS

❀ EUONYMUS

Enormously easy-going plants for sun or partial shade, there are two evergreen euonymus that will make an excellent job of smothering weeds. Brightly variegated 'Emerald 'n' Gold' creeps to no more than 60cm/2ft, with a spread of 90cm/3ft or more. White-edged 'Silver Queen' is even smaller, but will creep up a wall (to 1.8m/6ft) if there's one to hand.

❀ HEBE

As a general rule, it's the smaller leaved hebes that are the most hardy, and they make exceedingly neat little ground cover plants. 'Pagei' is one of the most popular, with small grey-green leaves and pure white flowers, to a height of 25cm/10in and a ground-hugging spread of 60cm/2ft or more. Grow hebes on well-drained soil, in full sun. Useful for chalky soils.

❀ HELIANTHEMUM (Rock rose)

Petite evergreens (rarely more than 15cm/6in), with a spreading habit, covered in papery, saucer-shaped flowers in June and July. Wonderful for a dry, sunny spot and experts at seeding themselves into paving cracks, where they can look very much at home. Lots of colours, from the bright to the pastel. Cut back hard after flowering, to keep them neat.

❀ LAVANDULA (Lavender)

Wonderful plants for a well-drained, sunny spot in any garden. Deep purple 'Hidcote' is one of the most

Lavandula stoechas

compact at 60cm/2ft, lighter purple 'Twickel Purple' rather taller. Slightly less hardy, but perfect for a sheltered spot, is the French lavender, *Lavandula stoechas*, each flower topped with 'rabbit's ear' purple bracts.

❀ POTENTILLA

The low-growing, shrubby

Euonymus *'Emerald 'n' Gold'*

Helianthemun *'Wisley Pink'*

Rhododendron yakushimanum

Spiraea *Golden Princess*

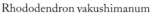

potentillas are great value, flowering from May right through to October. But if your garden's a sun-trap, avoid the reds and oranges, which can fade in extreme heat and/or drought. White 'Abbotswood' looks particularly fresh against the grey-green leaves, growing to 60cm/2ft with a spread of 90cm/3ft or more. Grow in well-drained soil, in sun.

❀ RHODODENDRONS & AZALEAS

The smaller rhododendrons and azaleas are particularly good in pots, using ericaceous compost to provide the acid conditions they need. The evergreen yakushimanum hybrids are especially compact, and very free-flowering. But they hate to get completely dry, so place them in a shady spot and water through any dry spells.

❀ ROSES

Of the many ground cover roses, 'Snow Carpet' is one of the daintiest, forming a low (30cm/1ft) mound studded with tiny white double flowers, spreading 75cm/2½ft. 'The Fairy' is taller and wider (at 60cm/2ft x 90cm/3ft), with arching stems and a constant supply of clear pink globe-shaped double flowers. To make the most of miniature and patio roses, plant them in groups, or pot them up so that they can really make an impact.

❀ SPIRAEA

The summer-flowering spiraeas are the best value for small gardens, from 'Little Princess' (a 60cm/2ft mound, covered in rose-pink flowerheads) to gold-leaved forms like green-gold 'Goldflame' and bright gold 'Golden Princess', both growing to around 75cm/2½ft. Give them good soil and full sun.

HARDY PERENNIALS

❀ ALCHEMILLA MOLLIS (Lady's mantle)

One of the perkiest, prettiest, easiest plants in all of gardening. Tight clumps of soft green scalloped leaves topped by a haze of tiny acid-yellow flowers, to 45cm/18in. Wonderful front-of-border plant for sun or partial shade, and can be kept fresh by cutting it hard back after flowering to encourage new growth.

❀ CROCOSMIA (Montbretia)

Sword-shaped leaves and long arching flowerspikes in fiery reds and oranges from summer to early

Crocosmia *Emily Mackenzie*

Hakonechloa macro '*Aureola*'

autumn. Lots to choose from, but we're fond of late-flowering 'Emily McKenzie', deep orange flowers with a mahogany throat to 60cm/2ft. Crocosmias must have sun and a well-drained soil, and in colder districts will benefit from the protection of a south-facing wall.

❀ FERNS

A wonderful group of plants for a shady spot. The native hart's tongue fern (*Asplenium scolopendrium*) has glossy, narrow flickering tongues, to 60cm or so. The soft shield fern (*Polystichum setiferum*) forms dense rosettes of lacy fresh green fronds to a height of 45cm/18in, and is virtually evergreen. Both, like the majority of ferns, appreciate a moist soil.

❀ GERANIUM

The true geraniums, which are quite unlike their bedding namesakes, are a beguiling lot, and you'll probably find yourself building up a collection. Tough, trouble-free and excellent weed-suppressors in sun or partial shade. And many of them flower over an exceedingly long period. Start with silver-pink 'Wargrave Pink', flowering from

June to September, and you'll soon be hooked on the whole family.

❀ GRASSES

Gold-striped *Hakonechloa macra* 'Aureola' is a lovely shaggy grass, turning rusty red in autumn. For evergreen gold in moist soil, choose Bowles' golden sedge, *Carex elata* 'Aurea', a densely-packed fountain of slim leaves. Both grow to 40cm/16in. Another excellent little evergreen is *Festuca glauca*, forming fat hedgehog cushions of blue-grey needles to little more than 15cm/6in. All are best in sun.

❀ HEUCHERA

Ground-hugging, weed-defying plants that divide sharply into two groups. The first are noted for their flowers – airy sprays of coral, red, pink or white, to 45cm/18in, for two or three months in summer. The second group are grown for their foliage colour. Deep plum-purple 'Palace Purple', for instance, and pewter-marbled 'Pewter Moon'. They thrive in sun or partial shade on any well-drained soil but dislike heavy clay.

❀ HOSTA

Superb plants, even though slugs love them as much as we do. Huge rosettes of lance-shaped or fatly rounded leaves, with some beautiful textures and colours, to an average height of 60cm/2ft. Lovely for combining with ferny or sword-leaved plants. No special recommendations, because they are all good. Grow in sun or shade, in any soil – the only thing they hate is dry soil combined with full sun. To keep slugs at bay, surround the emerging shoots with a thin layer of coarse gravel or crushed eggshells.

Hosta '*Francee*'

Jacob's ladder

Sedum spectabile *'Brilliant'*

❀ NEPETA (Catmint)

A mist of aromatic grey-green foliage, topped with a haze of lavender-blue flowerspikes, to around 60cm/2ft, from May through to September. Lovely edging plants, and especially pretty with roses. 'Six Hills Giant' is the tallest and most vigorous. Fine in any well-drained soil, and best in sun.

❀ PULMONARIA (Lungwort)

Double value. Spring flowers in a range of colours from white through pink and blue to red, followed by a wonderful summer display from the leaves. These make low, dense rosettes which, in our favourite forms, are heavily spotted or splashed with white. Best in shade, on any but a dry soil.

❀ SEDUM (Ice plant)

The 'ice plant' sedums are those with the attractive rosettes of fleshy, grey-green leaves and a grand display of cushion-shaped flowerheads (to 30cm/12in or so) in autumn. Bright rose-pink 'Brilliant' and crimson-pink 'Ruby Glow' are two of the best. Especially useful for dry soils, in full sun.

❀ STACHYS LANATA /BYZANTINA (Lamb's ears)

A wonderful evergreen edging plant for well-drained soil in full sun, forming dense mats of silvered woolly leaves, with spikes of wool-covered magenta flowers in summer. Neatest of all is non-flowering 'Silver Carpet', which grows to little more than 15cm/6in, with a spread of 60cm/2ft.

❀ THYMUS (Thyme)

The carpeting thymes are especially useful in the small garden. Compact, aromatic mounds that can be tucked into any sunny spot, with an interesting range of leaf and flower colour. 'Porlock' and 'Annie Hall' will both give a good show of pink flowers; for foliage, try bright golden 'Anderson's Gold' and silver-white 'Silver Queen'. Best in well-drained soil, and excellent for pots and between cracks in the patio.

Pulmonaria *'Munstead Blue'*

Best MEDIUM-SIZED PLANTS

All of these plants will grow equally well in pots and tubs.

SHRUBS

❀ ABELIA × GRANDIFLORA

A nicely arching semi-evergreen, and great for late summer colour, with clusters of fragrant pink and white flowers from July to October, to 1.8m/6ft or so. In the south and west, it can be grown in full sun in a sheltered part of the garden, but elsewhere it needs the protection of a sunny wall. 'Francis Mason' is a pretty, gold-variegated version.

❀ ACER (Maples)

The Japanese maples are horribly expensive, but utterly beautiful, and look wonderful in pots in partial shade where the delicate leaves won't be scorched by the sun. Two favourites: *Acer japonicum aureum* (now, irritatingly, *Acer shirasawanum aureum*) – for its neat fan-shaped golden leaves, and *Acer palmatum dissectum* 'Garnet', which makes a wide mound of feathery crimson-purple. Both will take an age to reach even 1.2m/4ft.

❀ BAMBOOS

Excellent, elegant screening plants, but the Latin names are a nightmare, and as they've recently all been changed (again), we'd advise that you simply choose one that grows to your required height. They're especially good for large pots, because it can be difficult to control their spread in the open garden. Keep moist, in sun or partial shade.

❀ BERBERIS

The whole berberis group is well worth investigating, because they're so easy to please. Of the coloured-leaf varieties, *Berberis stenophylla* 'Claret Cascade' is one of the most striking, an evergreen form with gracefully arching stems. The spring growth is wine purple, aging to green-purple – lovely against the small orange flowers. Grows slowly to 1.5m/5ft and colours up best in sun.

❀ CHOISYA TERNATA (Mexican orange blossom)

Thoroughly good tempered, domed evergreen with aromatic, fingered leaves and abundant, orange-scented white flowers in early summer and sporadically through to autumn. 'Sundance' is an excellent gold form. Grow in sun or partial shade. Reaches 1.8m/6ft.

❀ CORNUS (Dogwood)

If you want a bonfire of colour in the garden, place a *Cornus alba* where it will be caught by the low winter sun. This is the form of dogwood noted for its shiny, coloured bark, making great bristling stands to 1.5m/5ft. Of the red-barked varieties, 'Sibirica' has the best stem colour, but 'Elegantissima' has the bonus of delightful white-

Choisya ternata *'Sundance'*

Elaeagnus pungens *'Limelight'*

Magnolia x soulangeana

variegated foliage. Cut out a third of the stems each spring to encourage bright young growth.

❀ ELAEAGNUS

Tough, large-leaved evergreens for sun or partial shade, growing to around 2.4m/8ft. 'Maculata' is the most colourful, the dark green leaves heavily splashed with gold, 'Limelight' a more subtle yellow and lime green. 'Gilt Edge' is a good investment, the leaves outlined in gold. Remove any stems which revert to plain green.

❀ MAGNOLIA

Neatest of all this lovely group is *Magnolia stellata*, which takes years to creep to 2.4m/8ft or so. The starry white flowers, produced on bare spring branches, are sweetly scented. More imposing (at 10ft/3m) is *Magnolia x soulangeana*, with great goblet flowers in all shades from white to red-purple. Plant in a sunny, sheltered spot and enrich the soil liberally with organic matter.

❀ PHOTINIA

A remarkably chirpy evergreen, especially in the form 'Red Robin'. Lance-shaped glossy leaves, which emerge brilliant crimson and take an age to settle down to green. When that happens, just trim back lightly in midsummer to encourage new red growths. Best in a sunny spot sheltered from cold winds. Grows (slowly) to 2.4m/8ft, and tolerates a chalky soil.

❀ ROSES

For impact, we love the old shrub roses like warm pink 'Louise Odier' and 'Reine Victoria', but they can get pretty big, so the 'English' roses bred by David Austin are a very beautiful compromise. All the sumptuous blooms and glorious scents of the old varieties, on vigorous, well-clothed bushes in a range of heights from 60cm/2ft to 1.8m/6ft. In a small garden especially, they are a much more shapely choice than hybrid teas or floribundas.

❀ WEIGELA

Undemanding deciduous shrubs for sun or partial shade. The best for a small garden are those whose foliage will put on a good show after the early summer display of pink flower. The white-edged leaves of *Weigela florida* 'Variegata' (1.5m/5ft) are beautifully light and fresh, especially in shade.

❀ YUCCA

Architectural evergreens, excellent for pot growth, and splendid focal points. Those that form trunks can be a bit overpowering in a small space, so look out for *Yucca filamentosa* (1.8m/6ft in flower), with white thread-like leaf margins or the smaller *Yucca flaccida* 'Ivory' (90cm/3ft), both flowering from a young age. Grow in sun or partial shade.

Photinia fraseri *'Red Robin'*

HARDY PERENNIALS

HARDY PERENNIALS

❈ ACANTHUS
(Bear's breeches)

One of the most stately of border perennials, with tall spikes of white-hooded purple flowers to 1.2m/4ft in midsummer. The most free-flowering and handsome is *Acanthus spinosus*, with the large spiny, deeply divided leaves that the architects of Ancient Greece copied to adorn columns and pillars. Good in sun or light shade in fertile, well-drained soil.

❈ ANEMONE × HYBRIDA
(Japanese anemone)

These really are hard to beat for autumn colour, with attractive foliage and gold-centred flowers from August to October on tall wiry stems that need no staking. One of the tallest and loveliest, at 1.8m/4ft, is 'Honorine Jobert', a pure white single. They can be slightly invasive, increasing from underground stems, but the effort of clearing them back is a small price to pay. Best in sun, in fertile, moisture-retentive soil.

❈ ARTEMISIA (Wormwood)

A lovely group of silver-leaved plants, but they must have sun, shelter from cold winds, and a very well-drained soil. Cut-leaved *Artemisia ludoviciana* 'Silver Queen' and filigree 'Powis Castle', both to 90cm/3ft, are exceptionally pretty. Some artemisias are of dubious hardiness, but these two are very reliable.

❈ ASTILBE

These are lovely things and are ideal for a moist soil, in sun or shade. Ferny leaves and feathery plumes of flower to a height of 90cm/3ft. Colours range from deep crimson 'Fanal' through all shades of pink to a white beauty like 'Snowdrift'. They look especially good with the bold, broad leaves of hosta.

❈ CAMPANULA (Bellflower)

A tremendously varied family, ranging from low creepers to those that form great towering clumps. Of the latter, one of the loveliest is *Campanula lactiflora* (to 1.2m/4ft), topped with large heads of open bells. Soft pink 'Loddon Anna' and violet-blue 'Prichard's Variety' are two real winners. But don't stop there – any and every campanula is good news; long-flowering, easy to grow in sun (and some in partial shade), and very beguiling.

❈ EUPHORBIA

Another bunch of good guys. The most handsome of all is evergreen *Euphorbia wulfenii*, making great stands of 1.2m/4ft stems clothed in whorls of narrow, blue-green leaves, topped with broad domes of acid yellow flowers from May to July. For a dry, shady spot, the deeper green *Euphorbia robbiae* (25cm/18in) is perfect. But, again, explore the whole family – they're brilliant plants. The one drawback is that the sap is highly irritant, so always wear gloves when handling them.

❈ PAEONIA (Peony)

Yes, we know that the flowering period is very short, but peonies are such glorious things that we urge you to find space for their average height and spread of 90cm/3ft. And

Acanthus spinosus

Campanula lactiflora *'Prichard's Variety'*

Euphorbia characias ssp wulfenii

besides, the deeply-cut foliage is attractive in its own right, and colours up well in autumn. To give of their best, they need a fertile, moist (but not soggy) soil in sun or light shade.

✿ PHLOX PANICULATA

Terrific midsummer colour from the clusters of flower atop tall (90cm/3ft-ish) stems, in sun or partial shade. Wide range of colours in the red/pink/white/blue spectrum. Very long-lived and reliable, so long as they're in fertile, moisture-retentive soil; on lighter soils, water them through any prolonged hot, dry spells.

TIPS

✔ *In a moisture-retentive soil in sun or partial shade, the day lily (*Hemerocallis*) will give you a constant succession of summer flower. But do keep the succulent spring foliage protected from slugs.*

✔ *The shrubby willows are well worth investigating, with a wide variety of colour and form. Two of the best are* Salix lanata *for its thickly felted silver-white leaves, and purple-stemmed* Salix hastata *'Wehrhahnii' with its pure white woolly catkins. Neither grows to much more than 1.2m/4ft.*

✔ *Achilleas are remarkably long-lived, easy and decorative hardy perennials. Bright gold 'Gold Plate' will reach 1.2m/4ft without needing staking, and silvery-leaved 'Coronation Gold' grows to no more than 90cm/3ft. All achilleas make excellent dried flowers.*

Hemerocallis *'Chinese Coral'*

Phlox paniculata *'Mary Fox'*

Best LARGE PLANTS

All of the following plants will also be perfectly happy in large pots and tubs. Most won't achieve the height they would in the open ground – trees in particular will reach only about half their potential height.

TREES

❀ ACER (Maple)

Splendid family of trees. Three of the best for a small garden are *Acer pseudoplatanus* 'Brilliantissimum' (a beautifully neat lollipop with shrimp-pink young leaves maturing through yellow to dark green), *Acer griseum* with peeling, cinnamon coloured bark and fantastic autumn colour, and *Acer pensylvanicum*, the jade green bark vertically striped with silvery-white. All grow to 4.5-6m/15-20ft, in sun or partial shade.

❀ BETULA

Most birches eventually become pretty tall (12m/40ft +), and their shallow roots rob surrounding plants of moisture, so we wouldn't recommend them for open-ground plantings in very small gardens. But it's perfectly possible to grow them in large tubs or half-barrels, which restrict their growth without sacrificing one ounce of their beauty. All are good, in sun or partial shade.

❀ MALUS (Crab apple)

Any of the crab apples will do you proud in a small garden. One of the neatest is 'Red Jade' (to 3.6m/12ft), the weeping branches bearing white blossom and bright red fruits which hang on well into winter. 'Royalty' (6m/20ft) is notable for its glossy, rich purple foliage. 'John Downie' is far and away the best for crab apple jelly. Must have sun.

❀ PRUNUS

Two lovely cherries. *Prunus cerasifera* 'Nigra' (to 7.5m/25ft) is one of the most dramatically dark of all trees, a deep black-purple that looks wonderful with gold and bronze companions. *Prunus serrula* (6m/20ft) has willow-like leaves and spectacular bark of gleaming polished copper-red. Both prefer a sunny spot.

❀ ROBINIA

The golden *Robinia pseudoacacia* 'Frisia' is one of the most graceful of all trees – a light, billowing froth of acacia-like leaves to 9m/30ft or more. Useful on a dry soil, it's best in a sunny position. Plant where it's sheltered from high winds which can break the brittle branches. It can, we confess, tend to sucker, but removing them is a small price to pay for such a beauty.

❀ SORBUS (Rowan)

Rowans give superb value in the small garden. Spring blossom, attractive ferny leaves, brilliant

Acer griseum

Robinia pseudoacacia *'Frisia'*

TREES

Sorbus vilmorinii

autumn colour and berries through autumn and winter. 'Joseph Rock' is one of the most handsome, at 6m/20ft, and the primrose berries are thankfully left alone by birds. *Sorbus vilmorinii* is a little (3.6m/12ft) treasure, the berries aging from red to white. Grow in sun or partial shade.

SHRUBS

❀ BUDDLEIA
Often overlooked because it can be such a scruff if left unpruned, this is a graceful, valuable shrub for a sunny spot. Our all-time favourite is 'Lochinch', the arching stems tipped with long blue-lilac flowerspikes against grey-green leaves, to a height of 3m/10ft. To prune, cut back all stems to within two or three buds of the base in March.

❀ CAMELLIA
Noted for their delightful spring flowers, camellias are also excellent framework shrubs, providing a background of dense, glossy leaves

through the rest of the year, to 1.8-2.4m/6-8ft. They dislike chalky (limy) soils and do best in partial shade, in a sheltered position away from morning sun. Rich pink peony-flowered 'Anticipation' is especially pretty, and 'Alba Plena' is a fine double white.

❀ COTINUS COGGYGRIA
Commonly known as the smoke tree, this is in fact a rounded shrub to 1.4m/8ft or more, the 'smoke' coming from the feathery sprays of tiny flowers in July. The purple-leaved forms are outstanding – red-purple 'Notcutt's Variety' and deep plum-purple 'Royal Purple' are two of the best, the small rounded leaves taking on bright red tints in autumn. Tough and easy to grow, in sun.

❀ FATSIA JAPONICA
Best known as a houseplant, fatsia is perfectly hardy in all but the coldest districts, and it's a fabulous plant when liberated from a pot. Huge, fingered glossy leaves on a domed shrub to 3m/10ft. An easy to grow evergreen and fine in sun, but also tremendously useful for quite deep shade.

❀ HYDRANGEA
A great plant for a shady spot in reasonably moist soil, where it will grow large and lush and give a wonderful display of long-lasting flowerheads. The tall (to 2.4m/8ft) 'villosa' types are especially striking, with large white flowers surrounding the tightly packed blue-purple inner florets.

SHRUBS

Cotinus coggygria *'Royal Purple'*

SHRUBS

❀ LAVATERA 'BARNSLEY'

An enthusiastic, head-turning flowerer. 'Barnsley' has shot to fame over the past few years for its ability to reach 1.8m/6ft high and round in a single season, and for its mass displays of pale pink, red-throated hollyhock flowers from July to the first frosts. Grow in sun and cut back to within 30cm/1ft of the ground in late March to keep it within bounds.

❀ MAHONIA

Tough, stately, architectural evergreens, to 2.4m/8ft or more. 'Charity' is one of the very best, with the typical tiered sprays of holly-like leaves and, in winter, a topknot of sweetly scented yellow flowerspikes. Mahonias will grow in sun, but are particularly useful for shady areas.

Sambucus racemosa *'Plumosa Aurea'*

Lavatera *'Barnsley'*

❀ PIERIS

A superb evergreen shrub for an acid soil, or to grow in large pots in ericaceous compost. 'Forest Flame' has all the virtues of the family. A tall upright shrub to 3m/10ft, which in spring is a cascade of bright red young growth, fading through cream to green and, to cap it all, long dangling sprays of white lily-of-the-valley flowers. Quite a show-off. Prefers a slightly moist soil and must be grown in partial shade (it fries in sun).

❀ SAMBUCUS (Elder)

Common old elder? You'll be surprised at what it can do. *Sambucus nigra* 'Guincho Purple' is deep black-purple, *Sambucus nigra laciniata* a feathery cut-leaved green. For fringed golden foliage, there's *Sambucus racemosa* 'Plumosa Aurea' for a shady spot, 'Sutherland Gold' for sun. Quick growing, trouble-free beauties for any soil, in a range of heights from 2.4-4.5m/12-15ft. For best foliage colour prune out a third of the old wood in spring.

Pieris *'Forest Flame'*

Cupressus macrocarpa *'Goldcrest'*

Juniperus scopulorum *'Skyrocket'*

❀ VIBURNUM

A hugely varied group of plants, from winter-flowering evergreens to summer-flowering deciduous varieties. All are good but deciduous *Viburnum sargentii* 'Onondaga' is a real show-stopper. Deep bronze young leaves topped, in May and June, by lace-cap flowerheads of large pale pink flowers around a cushion of tiny bronze-pink florets. Easy to grow, in sun or partial shade, to a height of 1.8m/6ft.

CONIFERS

Conifers are such densely solid plants that they can be overwhelming in a small garden, but the following columnar varieties take up very little horizontal space and will fit in well.

❀ CHAMAECYPARIS LAWSONIANA 'Columnaris'

A narrow blue-grey spire to 1.8m/6ft after ten years (and ultimately to 6m/20ft or more). It grows well in any soil, so long as it's reasonably moist but free-draining, in full sun or partial shade.

❀ CUPRESSUS MACROCARPA 'Goldcrest'

One of the faster-growing conifers, making a broad golden-yellow column to 2.4m/8ft in ten years, and over 6m/20ft at maturity. Good in any soil, in full sun. And as one of us knows to her cost, they need very firm staking to counteract their tendency to keel over. A bonus is that the prickly foliage is lemon-scented.

❀ JUNIPERUS SCOPULORUM 'Skyrocket'

An exceedingly slim pointed rocket, with blue-grey foliage, to 1.8m/6ft in ten years, with an ultimate height of 4.5m/15ft or more. It looks especially effective taking off from a low planting scheme, or as a narrow flanking for a path. Fine in sun or partial shade.

❀ TAXUS BACCATA 'FASTIGIATA' (Irish yew)

A deep green column of densely packed foliage which slowly grows to around 1.5m/5ft in ten years (and ultimately to 4.5m/15ft). Yews are one of the hardiest of all plants, in any soil, and can be grown in full sun or deep shade. Plants can be clipped over to keep them extra-neat.

TIPS

✔ *Upright conifers are very vulnerable to snow damage – a heavy fall can cause stems to splay and split. So always knock the snow off, or tie in the branches with wire (ugly at first, but new foliage soon hides it).*

✔ *Sword-leaved phormiums and fountaining cordylines make wonderful focal points in a small garden, but both are tender, so are best grown in pots and overwintered in a cool room or frost-free greenhouse.*

✔ *Cornus 'Eddie's White Wonder' is a marvellous small tree/shrub, covered in large white 'flowers' (actually they're bracts, surrounding tiny flowers) in spring. The red-purple autumn leaves are attractive too.*

Best of the EDIBLES

HERBS

HERBS

With very few exceptions (noted in the text), all these edible plants are easy to grow in containers.

❀ BASIL

One of the strongest-flavoured of all herbs, and one of the trickiest to grow. A tender annual, it hates any hint of cold, so give it a sunny, sheltered position. Water in dry weather, but let it dry out between waterings. Pinch out regularly to keep bushy and remove any flowers. The small-leaved Greek basil has the best flavour.

❀ CHIVES

Neat, indestructible clumps of reed-like leaves and mauve pompon flowers that are also edible. This is great as an edging plant. Can be grown in sun or partial shade and is best in a moist soil although it happily tolerates a drier one. Lift and divide the clumps every three or four years.

❀ DILL

A fine-leaved annual with a delicate caraway/aniseed flavour, growing to 90cm/3ft. The leaves are especially good in salads and with fish, the seeds and tiny flowers in pickles. Easy to grow from seed sown outdoors in March and April – a once-only operation since they produce numerous seedlings. Grow in a sunny spot.

❀ FENNEL

Similar in appearance to dill and although rather taller at 1.2m/4ft or more, the airy haze of leaves won't block the view. A perennial that needs only a sunny spot to do well, it's much easier to grow than its bulbous relative, Florence fennel. The bronze-leaved form is exceptionally pretty, but not so strongly flavoured as the green.

❀ MINT

Mint is one of those plants that has its heart set on world domination, spreading rapidly on running roots. So in a small space it's safer to grow it in a pot. Place it in shade, and provide moister-than-average conditions by setting a saucer under the pot in summer. Applemint and spearmint are the best-flavoured for cooking, but

Basil

other forms, some of them attractively variegated, are a tasty addition to salads.

❀ PARSLEY

The secret of growing parsley successfully is to keep the ground moist during and after germination (if you're growing from seed), and to water well through any dry spells in summer. Grow in sun or partial shade – the latter will give more protection against drying out. For the best plants, sow or plant afresh each year. Flat-leaved French parsley is more vigorous than curly-leaved varieties, and has a much better flavour.

❀ ROCKET

Rocket's unique flavour – a mix of nuttiness, oiliness and spiciness – has made it the 'in' herb of the decade, helped along by Delia Smith. It really is delicious in salads, and very easy to grow from seed started in seed trays or *in situ*, in moisture-retentive soil. The flavour is hottest in sun, milder in partial shade. Cut regularly to prevent it from going to seed.

❀ ROSEMARY

With its informal spires of silver-backed needles and pretty blue flowers, rosemary is a highly attractive and useful evergreen for your small space. It grows to about 1.2m/4ft. Grow in well-drained soil in a sunny, sheltered position or, in colder districts, against a sun-warmed wall, and cut back any straggly or overlong shoots in spring. The only variety to be wary of is 'Prostratus' – a fine small plant but less hardy than the rest.

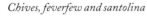

Chives, feverfew and santolina

Fennel

Purple sage

✿ SAGE

Another good evergreen shrub, forming a low dome and relishing the same conditions as rosemary. Purple and variegated forms are just as tasty as the plain grey-green, although the exceedingly pretty 'Tricolor' (variegated pink, white and purple) isn't reliably hardy. Trim over in spring to keep plants densely bushy, though they inevitably become leggy and woody in time, and should be replaced.

✿ TARRAGON

The edible member of the artemisia family, tarragon needs a warm, sheltered position and is best on a light, well-drained soil. If you can't provide this, grow it in pots using John Innes No 2 and add a little extra grit. French tarragon has the premium flavour, but can deteriorate after a few years. To replace it, sever a few of the running roots in spring and transplant them.

✿ THYME

Culinary thymes aren't as showy as those that we grow for their leaf colour or flower power, but they're excellent little aromatic evergreens all the same. Common thyme, *Thymus vulgaris* is the best all-rounder for cooking, followed by lemon-scented *Thymus citriodorus* (silver- and gold-variegated varieties available). For salads, try the interesting caraway flavour of *Thymus herba-barona*. Grow in sun, on well-drained soil, and trim lightly after flowering to encourage new growth and keep plants compact.

Parsley

FRUIT

Blackberry 'Loch Ness'

Single cordon pears

FRUIT

❀ APPLES

There are several options if you want to grow apples in a small space. Those grafted onto the dwarfest rootstock (M27) will grow to no more than 1.5m/5ft, though you must give them an extra-rich soil to compensate for the roots' lack of vigour, and keep them staked. An M9 rootstock will give you a slightly more vigorous tree, to around 2.4m/8ft. In the narrowest of spaces, grow the columnar Minarette and Ballerina trees, or cordons and espaliers which can be set against a wall or used as a living, fruitful fence.

All apples, apart from the new self-fertile 'Cox's Orange Pippin', need another tree nearby that blooms at the same time, for cross-pollination. Garden centres and nurseries have charts to guide you. Grow in sun, on a fertile soil that doesn't get too wet in winter or dry in summer.

'Cox's Orange Pippin'

❀ BLACKBERRIES

We tend to think of blackberries as huge rampant thickets, but when neatly trained against a wall, they take up very little ground space. One of the most decorative (and very fruitful) varieties is cut-leaved 'Oregon Thornless'. 'Loch Ness' (also thornless) is an upright, non-rambling variety that can be trained against a fence. Full sun is best, but partial shade is acceptable. Not recommended for pots.

❀ PEARS

Like apples, pears need another variety for cross-pollination, and a sunny, sheltered position in good soil. They much prefer a mild climate, though 'Hessle', from Yorkshire, is one of the most rugged of all. There's a wide range of varieties grafted onto 'Quince C' rootstock which restricts their height to around 2.4m/8ft, plus cordons and columnar Minarette trees (see apples). Recently introduced 'Patio Pears' are ideal.

Tomatoes

❀ CARROTS

Best on a light soil, in sun, home-grown carrots are delicious. Stump-rooted varieties and finger-carrot 'Suko' will also do well in pots and boxes. To deter carrot fly, which sniff them out and deposit their tunnelling larvae, thin out seedlings in the evening when they're less active, and grow a few spring onions nearby to put them off the scent.

❀ SALAD LEAVES

Lettuce first, and the most space-saving varieties are the tasty cos 'Little Gem' and the loose-leaf types which can be harvested a few leaves at a time rather than lifted. Young spinach plants, spring onion tops and curly-leaved endives can be harvested in the same way. Mild-flavoured corn salad (lamb's lettuce) and crunchy purslane will add interest to winter salads. All grow happily in pots.

❀ TOMATOES

Tomatoes, provided they're well-fed and evenly-watered, will give prolific crops. Grow them in pots, growbags or the open garden, in a sunny position. Bush types sprawl and flop about, so cordon varieties are best for small spaces. Simply tie them to a tall cane and take out all sideshoots. In taste tests, the most popular are usually the cherry-sized red 'Gardener's Delight' and orange-yellow 'Sungold'. For larger fruits we like 'Alicante'. But most home-grown taste great – the only one to avoid is 'Moneymaker', which has all the flavour and texture of a cotton-wool ball.

❀ STRAWBERRIES

The most compact and highly-prized fruit crop of all, growing happily in hanging baskets and pots or in the open garden. Enrich garden soil before planting and use a good multipurpose compost in containers. Best in sun, they dislike over-moist soils. Replace every three years, when fruiting starts to diminish. Twice-cropping 'Aromel' and 'Mara des Bois' have excellent flavour.

VEGETABLES

❀ BEANS

Runner beans take up very little horizontal space, so they're a useful crop if you've a spare piece of sunny wall with fertile, moisture-retentive soil, and can also be grown in a large pot or barrel on a wigwam of bamboo canes. Dwarf French beans are even easier, producing delicious pencil pods in any sunny piece of ground, and even in pots and window boxes.

TIPS

✔ *When you're browsing through seed catalogues, look out for 'mini vegetables' such as 'Bambi' cauliflower, 'Mini Iceberg' lettuce, aubergine 'Bambino' and sweet pepper 'Jingle Bells' – the latter two are ideal for pots.*

✔ *Yellow-fruited tomatoes are the most decorative of all, and both 'Golden Sunrise' and 'Yellow Perfection' are well-flavoured and easily grown outdoors. And though it's rather more orange than yellow, 'Sungold' is colourful and particularly tasty.*

✔ *Herbs such as rosemary, sage and fennel are a fine addition to a sunny mixed border, and chives make bright, neat edgings.*

Runner beans

Troubleshooting

One of the great things about small gardens is that problems tend to be on a smaller scale too. Once you've beaten back the initial invasion of weeds, they can easily be kept in check with a combination of mulches and plants (see pages 87–90). Pests and diseases will be minimal if your plants are growing strongly and well. And the rather more modern problem of garden security can be solved by taking a few sensible precautions. So with a bit of luck, these should be the least thumbed pages of the entire book!

PESTS AND DISEASES

Although it might sound a bit glib, the best method of pest and disease control is to prevent the problem from occurring in the first place. Good growing conditions, vigilance and cleanliness are the most powerful weapons in the P&D war.

Get off to a flying start by choosing sturdy, vigorous plants with no sign of pest or disease.

A strong-growing plant is much less likely to be attacked and seriously harmed, and the better your soil, the happier your plants are likely to be. So pamper your soil. The chapter on `Plants and Planting', shows just how you can turn a poor soil into something wondrous, and we can't overemphasise how important it is to keep on adding organic matter to maintain its fertility.

When you're buying plants, pick the sturdy, vigorous ones and make sure that they look healthy, rejecting those with the any sign of pests or diseases. Check, too, that they're not pot-bound – a mass of roots emerging from the drainage holes is a sure sign that they're past the optimum stage for planting.

When it comes to planting, it's important to set plants in the right position. Camellias, for example, will hate a hot dry position; they'll struggle and become more susceptible to attack. Hebes, on the other hand, will think it a very choice place and thrive. And don't forget to water plants through any prolonged dry spells in their first year, to encourage deep, strong rooting.

Problems may still occur, even on the strongest plants, but the sooner you spot a problem the better.

Most pests and diseases are easy to deal with in the early stages and an occasional wander round the garden, admiring the plants, will soon reveal any lurking nasties.

It's also important to keep the garden as clean and tidy as possible. Plant debris and leaf litter are natural hiding places for slugs and snails, so should be cleared up. Diseased plant material should be burned or binned. Never put it on the compost heap because the resultant compost could transfer the infection to other plants.

There are other tricks too. Choose disease resistant varieties wherever possible. Vegetables and fruit, in particular, are targets for the breeders, who are coming up with ever more disease resistant strains. And cherish the local wildlife. Birds, frogs and hedgehogs will make a meal of a vast array of pests, so encourage them. Squirrels, of course, are quite another matter, digging up newly planted bulbs and ring-barking young trees, but firmly fixed netting or chicken wire will help to minimise the amount of damage they can do.

Smaller creatures can be just as beneficial as birds,

frogs and hedgehogs. Ladybirds, lacewings and their larvae prey on aphids, as do the larvae of hoverflies. The best way of attracting the lacewings is by growing plants rich in pollen and nectar, and the poached egg plant (*Limnanthes douglasii* – a pretty annual which is shown at the start of this chapter) is particularly effective.

ORGANIC, CHEMICAL AND BIOLOGICAL CONTROL METHODS

Organic gardeners are enthusiastic advocates of providing the best possible growing conditions for their plants, and they've an ingenious variety of ways of protecting them from attack. These range from physical barriers for low-flying carrot fly and smearing Vaseline around the rim of pots to keep slugs at bay, to trapping earwigs in pots of straw.

If a problem arises that can't be dealt with by simply picking off a few diseased leaves or removing a voracious caterpillar, and spraying is necessary, the chemicals they use all come from natural sources; pyrethrum insecticide, for instance, is made from the pyrethrum daisy.

Chemical controls are man-made compounds and have a valuable role to play in pest and disease control, especially if used in conjunction with other methods. But if, like us, you're concerned about their effect on the environment, use them only as a last resort, and target them to the plants that really need them rather than blasting the whole garden. And always follow manufacturers' instructions to the letter.

Biological controls are an exciting new development. Natural enemies of a wide range of pests are introduced into the garden, greenhouse or conservatory and give excellent results as evidenced by the number of commercial growers who now use them. These controls are available from garden centres, and are also advertised in gardening magazines for mail order customers. However, they are fairly expensive, so read the packet or accompanying leaflet carefully in order to make optimum use of them.

Winter moth

THE MOST COMMON PESTS

Aphids

Greenfly and blackfly are the commonest, but they do come in various shades of sludgy brown too. They're sap-sucking insects, which attack a wide variety of plants. Leaves and young shoots can be sticky and distorted, with groups of insects and their larvae clustered along the stems. To control them, squash them by hand, use a soap-based insecticide or spray with a pirimicarb product which spares most of the beneficial insects like ladybirds.

Caterpillars

Most caterpillars are specialists, sticking to a strict diet of, say, all cabbage or all gooseberry leaf. Leaves are eaten from the edge, often giving them a scalloped appearance, and plants can sometimes be stripped completely. To control them, pick off the caterpillars by hand, squash them and spray the plant with an insecticide containing permethrin. Or you could use a biological method: spray with *Bacillus thuringiensis*, a naturally occurring bacterium which only kills caterpillars.

Sap-sucking aphids, like these blackfly, can cause considerable damage to both ornamental and edible plants.

Cat control

Much as we love cats, we do appreciate that many non-cat owners consider them to be the biggest garden pest of all.

A couple of years ago we asked, through the pages of a gardening magazine, for cat deterrent ideas from cat owners who were also keen gardeners. We were swamped with letters, so here's a selection of the most popular ideas:

• Fix a 30cm/1ft high barrier of loose black netting on top of your perimeter walls or fences. The neighbourhood cats will jump onto it, feel insecure, and jump back off again.

• Most of the pungent cat deterrents sold by garden centres don't last long and can be an expensive option. Mothballs are cheaper and will last for about six weeks even if it rains. We received many glowing reports of how effective they are.

• Sonic cat deterrents seem to be the most efficient of all. An infra red detector monitors a fan-shaped area of 100 degrees and has a range of 12m/40ft. On detecting movement, it emits a high frequency sound that only cats can hear, which scares them off but doesn't harm them. However it is expensive, at around £45 for the battery operated model and an extra £16 or so for a mains adaptor.

• Cats are most attracted to newly turned soil, so deter them by putting in a forest of small sticks or covering the whole area with chicken wire or netting to protect seedlings and young plants.

Here comes trouble!

Slugs and snails

These are public enemy number one; they are voracious and dedicated vegetarians. Seedlings are snipped off at ground level, new shoots eaten as they emerge, holes appear in leaves, entire stems can be defoliated. Their calling card is a silvery trail of dried slime. To control them organically, protect individual plants with a circle of grit or thorny cuttings, or use traps like beer-filled margarine tubs sunk into the ground. Or use the (relatively expensive) slug killers based on aluminium sulphate. For a cheaper chemical control, scatter slug pellets thinly (10cm/4in apart) among the plants and replace every fortnight or after heavy rain. If you want to use a biological control method, try a nematode product that can be watered onto moist soil. It lasts six weeks and gives good control of slugs but doesn't affect snails.

Vine weevil

Bedding plants, in particular, are susceptible to vine weevil, and the first sign of attack (wilting) is usually the last, since the problem is caused by the vine weevil's larvae which eat roots wholesale. These are small (up to 13mm/½in long) white grubs with a brown head, which develop into a blackish, gold-speckled weevil – a slow-moving creature which will even climb walls to get at hanging baskets. To control them, remove and destroy any grubs spotted when potting up, and squash the adult weevils. The most effective treatment is to use a biological control containing naturally occurring nematodes which prey on the grubs. Water into the ground or pots in spring or late summer.

THE MOST COMMON DISEASES

Blackspot

Blackspot is most commonly seen on roses, but can attack a wide range of other plants, with black or brown spots developing on the leaves. To control it, pick off and destroy all affected leaves. If the problem continues, spray roses with Bio Systhane, other plants with Murphy Tumbleblite. Bordeaux mixture is an organic alternative.

Downy mildew

Attacks a wide range of plants and is most active during long damp spells, forming a grey-white coating on the undersides of leaves and a yellowing on the upper surfaces. To control it, improve drainage if

PESTS AND DISEASES

Blackspot on rose leaves

possible, and cut out and destroy affected material. Spray with Bordeaux mixture or Bio Dithane 945 if the attack is severe.

Powdery mildew

Affects many plants and thrives in warm dry weather. It's especially noticeable in autumn after a hot summer. Michaelmas daisies and some roses are particularly susceptible. A powdery coating appears on leaves, normally on the upper surfaces, and flowers and fruits can also be affected. To control it, add organic matter to light or dry soils to aid moisture retention and keep susceptible plants well-watered in dry spells. Cut out

Powdery mildew

and destroy severely affected material. Spray with Phostrogen Safer's Liquid Fungicide or Murphy Tumbleblite II if the attack is severe.

Sooty mould

This is a black sooty coating on leaves which is caused by `honeydew', a substance excreted by aphids, scale insects and other sap-sucking pests, which is then colonised by fungi. There is no long term damage to the plant but light is excluded from the leaves and they may die. Camellias and plums seem particularly prone. To control it, kill off the insects with Phostrogen Safer's Insecticide then, as far as possible, wash off the sooty deposits with slightly soapy water.

HOLIDAY CARE

With a bit of forward planning, your garden can virtually look after itself while you're away. Ideally, come to an arrangement with a kindly neighbour who is prepared to do some watering for you. Generously suggest that they help themselves to any mature fruit, vegetables and flowers – a friendly gesture that will also stop crops like tomatoes from going to waste and flowering plants from going to seed (plants like sweet peas have the infuriating habit of stopping flowering altogether if not picked regularly). Make life easy for the neighbour by getting the hosepipe and watering can out and suggesting that they should only really worry about watering bedding plants, vegetables, pots and hanging baskets.

   If your garden is going to have to fend for itself, there are a few jobs worth doing just before you go. Patrol the garden for any pests and diseases – dealing with them now will prevent a plague on your return. Hoe or dig out any weeds – it's amazing how quickly they grow and it's important that they don't go to seed while you're away. Move pots, hanging baskets and window boxes out of sunny spots and water them thoroughly. This will usually suffice for a week, but if you're away for longer, rig up a rudimentary watering device. Group the pots around a bucket of water which is raised up on bricks and using strips of capillary matting as a wick, place one end in the soil, the other on the bucket. Some of the bigger planters will need more than one wick, so experiment in advance.

   Finally, cut the lawn and edge it, then pack your bags – you've earned your holiday.

Garden security

Recent statistics suggest, glumly, that there is a one in twenty chance that you will have something stolen from your garden in the next two years. But it seems that most garden crimes are carried out by opportunist thieves, so a few simple preventative measures might well be enough to deter them.

SHEDS
Keep them locked. A tough pad bar (also called hasp and staple) fitted with a strong padlock and secured by coach bolts is recommended by the police as being the most effective way of securing a door. There's also the problem that most shed doors open outwards with the hinges exposed, and it's quite easy for thieves to unscrew them. So replace at least one of the screws with a coach bolt (a long bolt with a smooth head that can't be undone by a screwdriver or spanner). As an extra precaution, if the shed houses valuable machinery, you could buy a shed alarm. A detector is fitted to the shed door which when opened, sets off a bell inside the house. These kind of alarms cost little more than a half-way decent

For the ultimate in lawn mower security, use a heavy-duty wall-mounted padlock and chain.

garden spade, so could be a good investment. If your shed has a window which opens, fit a lock, and curtain any windows to hide the contents from prying eyes.

TOOLS
Do put them away – even though they may not be worth much, they could be used to assist a burglar to break into your house or shed.

LAWN MOWERS AND POWER TOOLS
Mark them with your post code. The more conspicuous the marking, the less desirable they will be to prospective thieves.

ADDITIONAL PRECAUTIONS
Adding trellis work to the tops of fences gives a garden more height and privacy, and makes a fragile and treacherous foothold for would-be burglars. It'll be even more of a hazard if you cover it in prickly plants like pyracantha, quince (*Chaenomeles*) or well-thorned roses. Finally, hanging baskets can be padlocked to their brackets, tubs and urns cemented in, and a few bricks at the base of larger planters will make them far too heavy to lift.

Finally, do check your insurance policy to find out what cover is provided for theft and vandalism in the garden – each company varies considerably.

Security lights which come on automatically when a movement is detected in the garden are a good deterrent.

Index